SPECTATOR SPORTS *Made* SIMPLE

How to Watch, Understand, and Enjoy

Baseball, Football, Basketball, Golf, Tennis, Soccer, Bowling, and Ice Hockey

DAN BARTGES

MASTERS PRESS
NTC/Contemporary Publishing Group

Library of Congress Cataloging-in-Publication Data

Bartges, Dan, 1948–
Spectator sports made simple : how to watch, understand, and enjoy baseball, football, basketball, golf, tennis, soccer, bowling, and ice hockey / Dan Bartges.
p. cm.
Includes index.
ISBN 1-57028-204-8
1. Sports. I. Title.
GV704.B37 1999
796--dc21 98-47087
CIP

Cover photographs copyright © PhotoDisc, Inc.
Cover design by Nick Panos
Interior design by Precision Graphics

Published by Masters Press
A division of NTC/Contemporary Publishing Group, Inc.
4255 West Touhy Avenue, Lincolnwood (Chicago), Illinois 60646-1975 U.S.A.

Printed in the United States of America
International Standard Book Number: 1-57028-204-8
99 00 01 02 03 04 05 06 QP 18 17 16 15 14 13 12 11 10 9 8 7 6 5 4 3 2 1

To my dad and grandad

CONTENTS

ACKNOWLEDGMENTS

I owe a stadium full of thanks to the following people for their time, encouragement, and sports knowledge: John Adams, Carleton Anderson, Michael Balestra, Matt Ball, Clyde Bartges, Michael Brooslin, Gary Brown, Jeff Butler, Hugh Campbell, Saleem Choudhry, Jimmy Connors, John Dalzell, Andy Davis, Bob Dewsbury, Nancy Egloff, Jeff Gettler, Ken Hart, Dawn Holgate, Len and Shirley Hollabaugh, Greg Inglis, Carla Johns, Dave Kelly, Leslie King, Michael Kammarman, Bruce Markusen, Bob McIver, Bill Melchior, Richard Merrill, Melody Metz, Randy Mobley, Jim Moorhouse, Debby Padgett, Lyn Ryman, Greg Solomon, Paul Wallo, Jennifer Walsh, Dell Warren, Mark Wesselink, Allen Wilhelm, and Ken Samelson and Chad Woolums of Masters Press, and to Julia Anderson of NTC/Contemporary Publishing Group.

To these organizations for their invaluable proofreading and expertise: American League, AMF, Inc., Association of Tennis Professionals Tour, Basketball Hall of Fame, D.C. United, International League, Jamestown-Yorktown Foundation, Ladies Professional Golf Association, Library of Congress, Major League Soccer, National Baseball Hall of Fame, National Basketball Association, National Bowling Hall of Fame and Museum, National Collegiate Athletic Association, National Football League, National Hockey League, Professional Golfers Association, Pro Football Hall of Fame, Professional Bowlers Association, Professional Women's Bowling Association, Richmond Renegades Hockey Club, U.S. Soccer Federation, United States Tennis Association, the University of Richmond's Athletic Department, and the Women's Tennis Association Tour.

I especially appreciate the constant support of my wife, Kelley.

INTRODUCTION

On a warm, summer evening 10 years ago, I attended my first stock-car race. It was at a small, vintage track called Southside Speedway, just outside Richmond, Virginia.

Sitting in the metal bleachers with a friend, I was bored and confused. All those roaring cars were racing and passing each other around the oval track, but it was impossible to tell which car was winning. Finally, I leaned forward, tapped the man sitting in front of me on the shoulder and asked, "How do you know which car is in the lead?"

I'll never forget his response. At first he looked incredulous, then suspicious, and then, apparently sensing my sincerity, he broke into a broad grin and asked, "Is this your first race?" "Really?" smiled his wife. Thrilled to have the opportunity to share their favorite spectator sport with a couple of novices, they pointed out the electronic sign at the far end of the track that showed three numbers, which periodically changed. Those were the numbers on the cars in first, second, and third place.

Instantly, the race became exciting.

The experience said something important about all spectator sports: a key insight can instantly transform one's attitude about an unfamiliar sport and make watching it a lot more enjoyable.

Each of the eight major spectator sports in this book appeals to millions of people for a very good reason—each is uniquely powered by strong currents of drama and suspense.

To plug into that excitement, simply learn the key aspects of the sport you're interested in. In that regard, I hope this book helps you as much as that racing fan and his wife helped me. It's designed to make you "spectator literate" about each sport after reading its respective chapter—which for most sports will take 15 to 20 minutes. It won't make you an expert, but it will enable you to enjoy watching the game and to ask informed questions.

The explanations of play action, rules, and strategies pertain to the professional level of each sport with the exception of basketball and football; those two chapters include both pro and collegiate rules.

Nothing Beats the Real Thing

As a spectator, you will probably watch most sporting events on television. Although TV's sports coverage is usually very good, there's just no substitute for attending a live event to gain a true appreciation for the sport you're interested in.

Here are two reasons why:

First, each sport is wrapped in its own sensory atmosphere that can only be appreciated "ringside." You haven't fully experienced professional ice hockey, for example, until you've sat in an arena, listened to the roar of the frenzied crowd, and witnessed the concussive impact of a player being slammed against the retaining wall. TV can give you instant replays, but it can't deliver that visceral impact. Yet, that aspect is intrinsic to the sport and helps define it.

Baseball is another good example. If you want to understand that sport, then attend a game, breathe in the night air, and eat a hot dog smothered in mustard and relish, a bag of peanuts, or a box of popcorn; look around at the happy faces of cheering couples and friends and at the little kids wearing baseball caps and gloves.

Once you've collected those experiences firsthand, your sensory memory will kick in to embellish all subsequent TV spectating.

Second, you will often miss a lot of the secondary—yet still important—play action on TV; the screen is simply not big enough to absorb all concurrent action of many sports. The TV camera can't take in all the action on a football field, for example, or on a hockey rink or a soccer field. Seeing these events firsthand enables you to understand what all the different players do and to better appreciate the dynamics of each sport.

In the final analysis, watching sports is about enjoying yourself. I once asked tennis great Jimmy Connors for three tips on getting the most out of watching tennis. His reply could apply to any sport in this book:

1. Have an appreciation for competition.

2. Have a cold drink and a hot dog.

3. Have a good time.

Part I

TEAM SPORTS

chapter one

BASEBALL

Baseball can be a deceptively simple sport to watch—a handful of guys standing around on a grassy field waiting for someone to hit the ball.

But this sport—because of its ingenious structure, its dramatic twists and subtle turns—has riveted fans to the edges of their seats for more than 150 years. Widely popular and culturally ingrained, baseball is often called "America's national pastime."

Basic Play

Baseball is played by two opposing teams of nine players each on a large, grassy playing field (well, not always; a third of major league fields are now carpeted with artificial turf). The teams alternate playing offensively and defensively. When Team A plays offense, it is said to be "at bat"—meaning that its players take turns trying to hit the ball with a wooden bat and then run around the bases to score points. Team B, meanwhile, plays defense "in the field," trying to catch the batted ball before it hits the ground or, with ball in hand, to tag out the runner before he scores (more on that later).

A game—which typically takes about three hours to play—is divided into nine periods called "innings." During an inning, each team is given a turn at bat while the other team assumes the defensive role of playing the field. The team at bat continues its attempts to score points (called "runs") until three "outs" are accrued against it by the opposing team. At that point, the teams switch roles—the team that had been batting plays the field.

The Playing Field

A regulation baseball field (see Figure 1) covers about two and one-third acres and is divided into the "infield" and the "outfield" areas. The playing field is enclosed by two white "foul lines" running at right angles from home plate. One line is drawn through first base and the other through third base with both of the lines extending all the way out to the high fence (or wall) that stretches across the outfield and defines the outfield's outer edge.

The first indoor ballpark, the Houston Astrodome, opened in 1965.

The infield is where most of the action takes place; it is contained within the red clay/dirt pathway connecting the four bases. The bases, which the players run in counterclockwise order, are "first base," "second base," "third base," and "home" (or "home plate"). The actual bases are square-shaped, white rubberized bags stuffed with padding, measuring 3 inches thick and 15 inches on each side. Home plate, about the same size as the other bases, is a five-sided slab of white rubber.

The bases are spaced 90 feet apart. To score a point ("score a run"), a player must advance around all of the bases. Depending on how the action develops, a player may advance in one continuous run or through a succession of base-by-base runs. Interestingly, once all the bases are run, a player will have traveled 360 feet, or 20 percent farther than the full length of a football field.

The squared layout of the four bases is called "the diamond." In the middle of the diamond is an 18-foot-diameter circle called the "pitcher's mound," the area from which the pitcher throws the ball in the direction of the other team's batter, who, standing beside home plate, attempts to hit the ball. A distance of 60 feet 6 inches

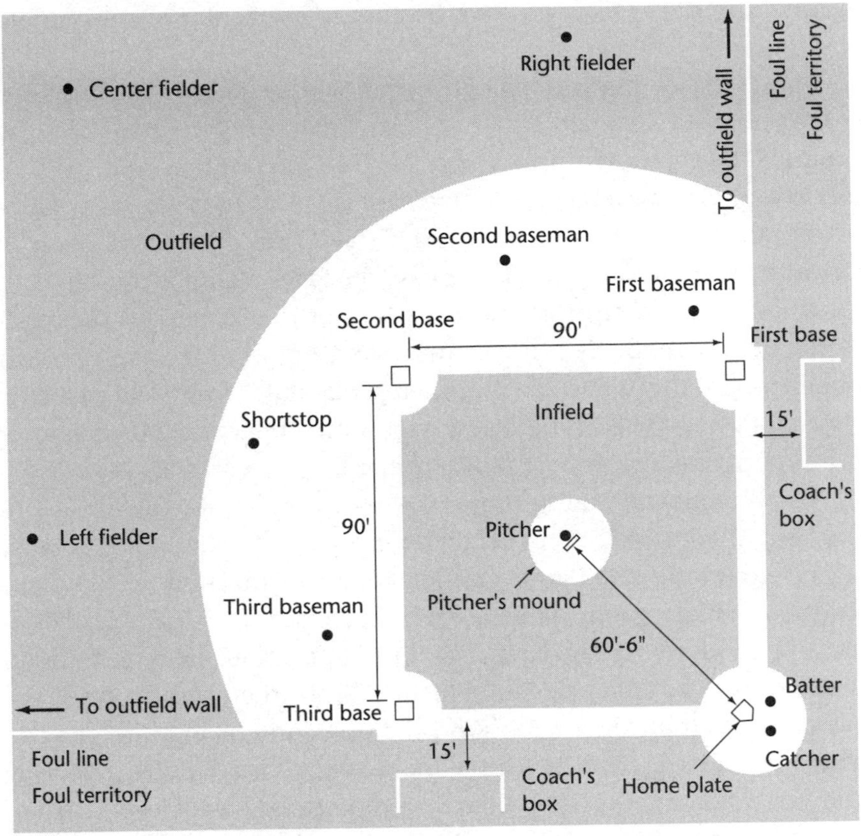

Figure 1. The baseball field consists of the outfield and infield areas, as well as four bases. In order to score a run for his team, the batter must hit the ball into "fair territory" (the playing area between the two foul lines) and run to all four bases in counterclockwise succession without being put out by the opposing team.

separates the middle of the pitcher's mound, called the "pitching rubber," from home plate.

The outfield is the open space between the outer edges of the diamond and the backfield fence or wall. Although the size of the outfield does vary somewhat from ballpark to ballpark, the distance from home plate to either the left or right edge of the outfield wall is on average about 330 feet, and the distance to the center of the outfield wall is about 400 feet.

If the batter hits the ball into the playing field—and provided that the ball isn't caught by an opposing player before it touches the ground—the batter will score a point if he can run around the diamond and touch each consecutive base with his foot while avoiding being put out by the opposing team (see "How 'Outs' Are Made"). Once the runner safely reaches a base, he faces a choice: he can wait safely on that base until the next batter hits the ball to advance him to the next base, or he can continue running on to the next base in hopes of making it there before being put out. (Only one player is allowed to occupy each base at any point in time, and a base runner is not permitted to pass a fellow runner.)

Balls hit all the way to the outfield—if they're not caught before they hit the ground "on the fly" for an instant out—will almost always guarantee the batter enough time to run safely to first base (called a "single"), and maybe even to second base (called a "double"), without being tagged out. If, by chance, the batter makes it all the way to third base, he's hit a "triple." If in the unlikely event the batter makes it all the way around the bases and back to home plate where he started, then he's hit a "home run," or a "homer," scoring one point for his team. A batter who hits the ball and runs safely to base is said to have gotten a "base hit."

Balls hit within the foul lines are deemed "fair balls" (because they land within "fair territory"). Only fair balls permit the batter to attempt to race to first base and any runners already on base to attempt to make it to the next base. If a ball is hit so far that it clears the outfield fence but still lands between the imaginary extensions of the two foul lines, it is judged a home run and automatically scores at least one run—that of the player who hit it—plus, like any home run, additional runs for each teammate already on base when the home run was hit. If a batter hits a home run when his team already has players on first, second, and third base, it is said that the "bases are loaded" and the home run, called a "grand slam" in this case, scores four runs. A grand slam is the biggest offensive play in baseball. Even though a home run scores at least one point automatically, the rules state that the home-run hitter still must run around all the bases as a mandatory formality. (Said baseball legend Babe Ruth, "I have only one superstition. I make sure to touch all the bases when I hit a home run.")

How "Outs" Are Made

As mentioned, the team at bat (Team A) must relinquish its offensive role once the opposing team (Team B) accrues three outs against it during one inning. Team A, now playing the field, cannot assume the offensive role again until it collects three outs against Team B. When both Team A and Team B have each had a turn at bat and in the field, a new inning begins.

Here are the four ways in which the defensive team can put out an opposing player.

The Batter "Strikes Out"

Each batter is given several opportunities to hit the ball thrown by the pitcher and to run for the safety of first base. If the batter swings his bat at the ball and misses it (which happens often), that counts against him and is called a "strike." If the batter collects three strikes in any one at-bat, his team is penalized with one out, and the next player comes to bat. If the batter elects not to swing at the ball, but in the opinion of the umpire (who stands behind the batter and the catcher) the pitch passes through the strike zone (see "Strike Zone," Figure 2), then the batter is also penalized one strike. If he hits the ball into foul territory, that also counts as a strike. There is an exception: if a batter already has two strikes against him and hits a foul ball, it is not counted as a strike or a "ball." Foul balls do count as a first or second strike, but a batter cannot strike out on a foul ball.

A pitch which does not pass through the strike zone is counted as a strike if the batter tries to hit it anyway and misses, or as a ball if the batter realizes that it's going to be out of the strike zone and wisely elects not to attempt to hit it. If a batter accumulates four balls while at bat, then he is automatically awarded a trip to first base at no risk of being put out. This is called a "walk," or "walking

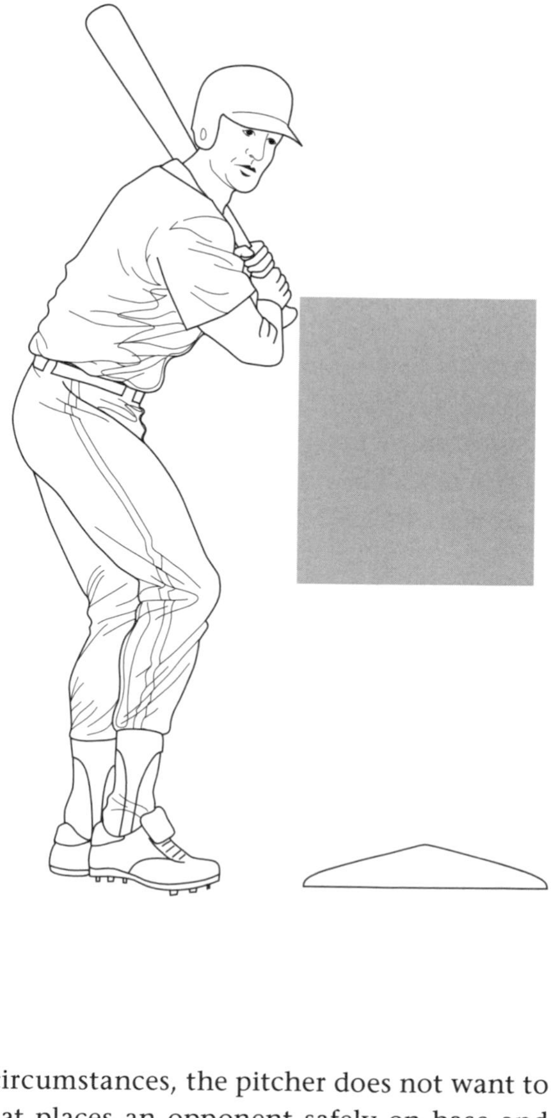

Figure 2. The pitcher usually tries to throw the ball through the "strike zone" (shaded area above home plate between the batter's armpits and knees). If the pitch passes through the strike zone, the batter tries to hit it. If he misses the ball, or if he decides not to swing the bat at all, it is counted as a strike against him. If the batter accumulates three strikes, he is counted "out." If, however, the ball passes outside the zone and is not swung at by the batter, it is called a "ball." If the batter accrues four balls, he is permitted to go to first base (he is "walked" to first base).

the batter." Under most circumstances, the pitcher does not want to walk a batter because that places an opponent safely on base and possibly in contention to score a run. If there is already a player on first base when the batter is walked, the player on first is permitted to advance to second (because only one runner is allowed on a base). A batter is also awarded a walk to first if he is hit by a pitched ball.

As a spectator, it's important to know "the count" on a batter—how many balls and strikes have accumulated at any point during his turn at bat—because the count will influence both offensive and defensive decisions. Before each pitch, the home plate umpire will signal the count with his fingers—left hand shows the number of balls, right hand the number of strikes—and the TV or radio commentator will usually state the count. If, for example, the pitcher is preparing to throw a pitch to a batter who already has accumulated three balls and one strike, it is called a "three-one pitch." The umpire or announcer might also say that the count is "three-and-one." A "full count" would represent "three-and-two," meaning the batter has accumulated three balls and two strikes, and the next pitch—unless fouled off—will decide the batter's fate. If a full count pitch is a strike, then the batter is out; if it's a ball, the batter walks to first base; if the ball is hit into fair territory, then the batter will attempt to reach base safely before being put out.

The Batted Ball Is Caught on the Fly

If the batter hits the ball into either fair or foul territory and a member of the opposing team catches the ball before it touches the ground, that counts as an automatic out against the team at bat.

The Runner Is Tagged Out

A runner will be ruled out if, while he is attempting to run from one base to the next, he is tagged by an opposing team member who is in possession of the baseball. If, however, the runner can make it to the next base without getting tagged, he is considered "safe" and remains on that base. (Note: The batter, running at full speed for first base, is permitted to overrun that base; if, however, he overruns second or third base, he can be tagged out by the opposition when not touching the base.)

The Runner Is Forced Out

There are two circumstances in which a runner must attempt to run to the next base. In these special situations, an opposing team member in possession of the ball does not need to touch (or "tag") the runner. The opposing team need only throw the ball to a teammate who must catch the ball and touch the base that the runner is headed for before the runner touches that base. Here are two situations in which a runner is forced to attempt to get to the next base and, therefore, is susceptible to a "force out":

1. Once the batter hits the ball into fair territory, he must attempt to race to first base before the opposing team can throw the ball to the first baseman. The runner will be called out if he fails to tag the base before the first baseman catches the ball (the first baseman must have a foot or hand on the base when he catches the ball).

2. If a player on the team at bat makes it safely to base, he will usually remain safely on that base until a teammate hits the ball into fair territory. He is permitted the option of either seeking the next base or, if he thinks the risk of being tagged out is too great, remaining on that base and waiting for a better opportunity. He must seek the next base, however, if his fellow teammate running the bases behind him seeks the same base he now occupies. Since two players can't occupy the same base at the same time, the lead runner is forced to seek the next base when the second runner seeks to take the base he occupies. In that forced situation, the opposing team need only throw the ball to a teammate who must catch the ball and touch the base before the lead runner reaches it. If the lead runner fails to "beat the throw," he falls victim to a force out.

Stealing Bases

There is a provocative provision in baseball that injects added tension and excitement into every game. It's called "stealing" a base.

When the pitcher is preparing to throw the next pitch, an opposing player already on first, second, or third base is allowed to take the risk of attempting to run to the next base. To foil this attempt, the defensive team must throw the ball to a teammate at that next base and tag the advancing player before he reaches the base. Usually, that throw will be made by the catcher; sometimes it is made by the pitcher. Many gutsy, fast-running players have become famous for their cunning ability to steal bases.

"I think there are only three things that America will be known for 2,000 years from now when they study this civilization: the Constitution, jazz music, and baseball. They're the three most beautifully designed things this culture has ever produced."

—Gerald Early, author and educator

If the batter hits the pitch and it is caught on the fly for an automatic out, then any player attempting to steal a base must "tag up." Tagging up means that a player must run back to the base that he previously occupied and touch it before he's allowed to try to advance again. After the fly ball is caught, the defensive team can attempt to throw the ball to the base before the runner tags up, in which case the runner will be called out. In essence, the farther the runner strays from his current base, the greater his chance of being "picked off" by a fast, accurate throw.

Base stealing is a risky move for the runner. At the same time, an aggressive player pushing to steal a base becomes a stressful distraction to both the pitcher and the catcher. All in all, stealing bases can be an effective way for the offensive team to advance its runners and score more runs while pressuring the opposition.

The Players

Each major league team has nine players on the field at any one time plus another 16 who sit in a waiting area called "the dugout" and can be used as substitutes. Although players' sizes vary, the average player is about six feet tall and weighs about 200 pounds; he is well trained for speed and strength. In the dugout, each team also has several coaches and one manager, who directs his team's play.

Of the nine players in the field, six play in the infield and three in the outfield. Here is a summary of the nine defensive positions (see Figure 3).

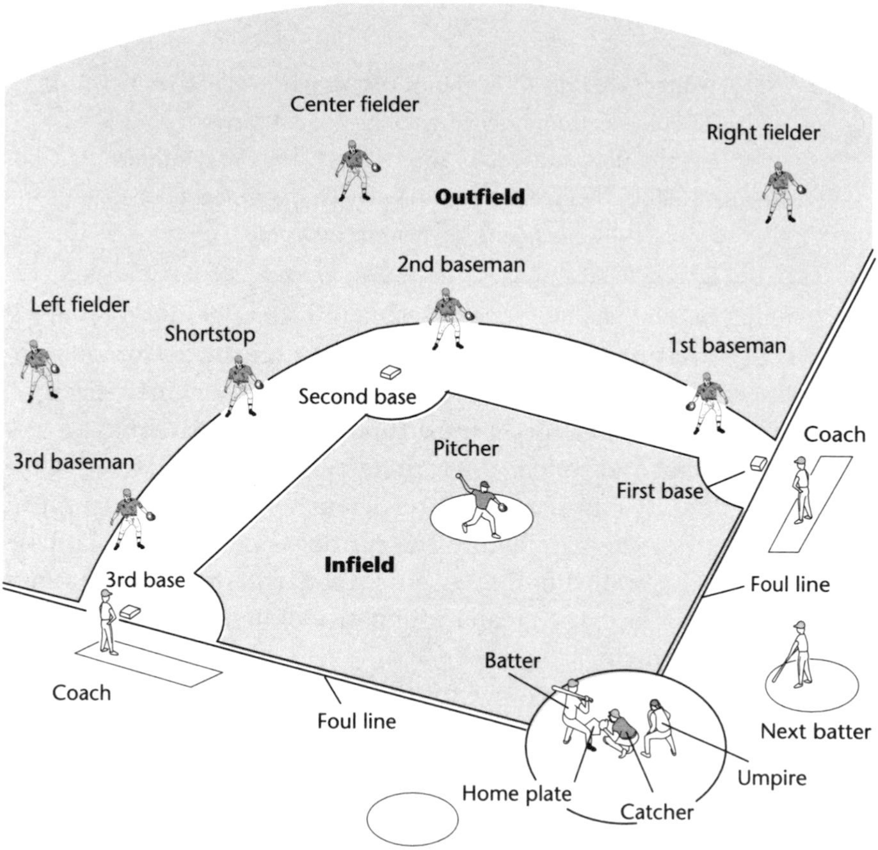

Figure 3. The nine field positions for the team playing defense are pitcher, catcher, first baseman, second baseman, third baseman, shortstop, left fielder, center fielder, and right fielder.

Pitcher

Delivering each pitch to the opponent's batter, the pitcher is considered the most important defensive player on the team. This player stands on the pitcher's mound in the center of the infield diamond and throws (or "pitches") the ball across home plate, where a player from the opposing team attempts to hit it. An effective major league pitcher is enormously talented at throwing a variety of pitches that are quite difficult to hit—for example, a fastball, a ball that curves to the right or to the left, a ball that dips down, or a change-up (a slow-pitch that appears to be faster than it really is) (see Figure 4). If a pitcher plays all nine innings of a game, he might throw 100 to 140

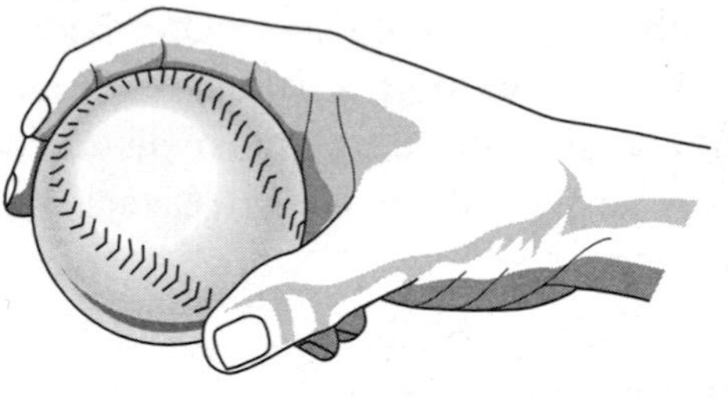

Figure 4. This is the baseball grip used by a pitcher to throw a fastball. Combined with various snaps and twists of the wrist as the ball is released, the pitcher makes slight adjustments to his grip in order to throw other types of pitches (curveball, knuckleball, slider, sinker, etc.).

pitches. Because pitching is so exhausting, in order to rest his arm the same pitcher does not play every game.

Catcher

Squatting behind home plate, this valuable player catches those balls thrown by the pitcher that the batter fails to hit. A good catcher is smart and has studied the strengths and weaknesses of each batter. He recommends certain pitches through secret hand signals to the pitcher. For example, he might signal for a fastball or a curveball or for the pitch to be thrown closer to the batter or farther away. In addition, the catcher must stay alert and have a strong arm to throw quickly to second base (127 feet from home plate) or third base (90 feet) to eliminate a runner trying to steal.

First Baseman

Standing a few steps to the left of first base, the first baseman's primary responsibility is to catch balls thrown to him by his teammates

---

On George Washington's birthday in 1936, the famous Walter "Big Train" Johnson visited the small Virginia town of Fredericksburg. The retired pitcher had been challenged to duplicate Washington's legendary feat of hurling a silver dollar across the Rappahannock River. In front of several thousand spectators, radio commentators, newspaper reporters, and movie cameras Johnson wound up and threw a coin overhand like a baseball pitch. Clearing about 100 yards of water, the silver dollar sailed across the river with a few feet to spare.

---

before the runner can tag first base. This player also catches batted balls that come into his immediate territory on the infield diamond. Because this field position is not as demanding as most defensive positions, first basemen are usually very good at batting (players usually excel at either fielding or batting).

Second Baseman

Standing a few steps behind and to the right of second base, the second baseman relies on speed and agility. He catches balls thrown to him by his teammates to put out runners before they reach second base and also catches (or "fields") balls hit by the batter that travel through his immediate territory on the infield diamond.

Shortstop

Guarding the open space between second and third bases—an area to which many balls are hit—the shortstop relies on exceptional quickness, agility, and defensive prowess to defend his immediate territory on the infield diamond. This player possesses a strong arm to get the ball quickly to the first baseman before the batter can reach base safely. He also sometimes covers second base.

Third Baseman

Standing just to the right of third base, the third baseman catches balls that have either been thrown to him by his teammates or hit hard into his immediate territory on the infield diamond. This player, like the shortstop, must have a strong arm to throw the long distance across the diamond and get the ball to the first baseman before the batter reaches base safely.

Left Fielder

Standing in the outfield area between second and third base, the left fielder attempts to catch batted balls before they touch the ground (called "fly balls") for an automatic out or to field balls that bounce along the ground (called "ground balls" or "grounders"). This player should possess a fairly strong arm to throw the ball to his infield teammates (usually the second or third baseman) in order to stop the runner's advance around the bases.

Center Fielder

Standing in the outfield area behind second base, the center fielder—like the left fielder—attempts to catch fly balls and to field ground balls. This player should possess adequate speed and quickness to cover a deeper, wider area of the outfield territory. He should also possess a strong arm in order to throw the ball to his infield teammates (usually the second baseman, third baseman, or shortstop) in order to stop the runner's advance around the bases.

Right Fielder

Standing in the outfield area between first and second base, the right fielder—like the other outfielders—attempts to catch fly balls and to field ground balls. This player generally possesses the strongest throwing arm in the outfield in order to throw the ball to his infield teammates (usually the shortstop or third baseman) in order to stop the runner's advance around the bases.

A Word About Umpires

The four officials on the field are the umpires, whose judgment serves as the final rule on all plays. All major league baseball games are officiated by professional, unbiased umpires paid by the leagues and not by the individual teams. Umpires generally wear dark slacks and light-colored, short-sleeve shirts or dark blazers.

The home plate umpire, whose job it is to decide whether each pitch is a ball or a strike, stands directly behind the catcher and wears a protective face mask and padded vest. He is also the official who determines whether or not a player running from third base toward home plate has beaten the throw and arrived safely to score a run.

The first, second, and third base umpires determine whether runners are safe or out in their attempts to advance to those respective bases. On occasion, the home plate umpire may be asked to rule on a play at first, second, or third base if one of the base umpires for some reason cannot make a decision on a play.

"Play Ball!"

Prior to a game, each team manager provides the umpire and the opposing team with a sheet stating the "batting order" of his players (called the "starting line-up"). Those listed players (or their substitutes) must bat in that specific order for the rest of the game. Once the starting line-up for each team has been exchanged, everyone in the ballpark—players, coaches, umpires, and fans alike—pauses for the singing of the national anthem. Immediately afterward, the home-plate umpire's familiar shout, "Play ball!," officially marks the start of the baseball game.

"Take Me Out to the Ball Game" is the most famous song about any American sport. Jack Norworth wrote the lyrics in 1908 while riding on a New York subway train and collaborated with tunesmith Al Von Tilzer to compose this ever-popular hit. (A star of vaudeville, Norworth and his equally famous wife, singer Nora Bayes, co-wrote "Shine On Harvest Moon.")

By protocol, the visiting team is always first to bat in each inning, followed by the home team. The first half of each inning is called the "top" of that inning; the second half—played by the home team—is called the "bottom" of that inning. An electronic scoreboard shows the score for every inning (see Figure 5).

Play begins with the lead batter, bat in hand, taking his position in a marked-off area beside home plate called the "batter's box." Squatting directly behind the plate is the catcher for the opposing team. Staring at him from just over 60 feet away is the pitcher, who decides what type of pitch might be most effective against the particular batter at the plate. The catcher makes pitching recommendations to the pitcher through a series of secret hand/finger signals. If the pitcher doesn't agree with the recommendation, he will shake his

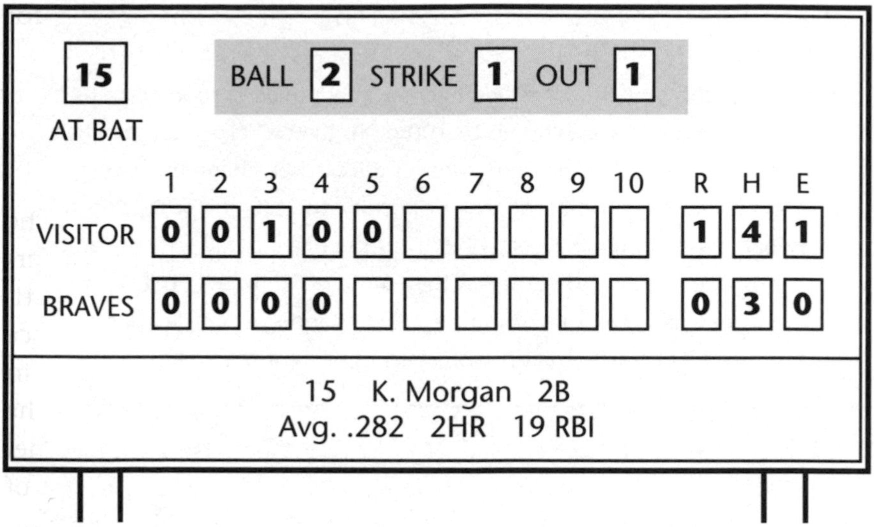

Figure 5. The electronic scoreboard in every major league stadium conveys very helpful information about what's going on in the game as well as background data on each player as he comes to bat. According to this sample scoreboard, the player at bat—K. Morgan, #15, who plays second base (2B), has a respectable batting average of .282, and has hit two home runs (2 HR) and batted in 19 runs (19 RBI) so far during the season—has a count of two balls and one strike against him; one out has been made against his team. The game is now in the bottom of the fifth inning (the second half of the fifth inning), and the score is 1–0. In the third inning, the visiting team scored the only run (R). There have been a total of seven hits (H) and one error (E).

head (called "shaking off the signal"), thereby asking for another suggestion from the catcher. All other players on the field stand in defense of their territory, poised for action.

The pitcher makes his decision, begins to deliver the pitch (called the "windup"), and hurls the baseball toward home plate. At that moment, the batter has less than half a second to make some very important calculations. First, he must try to determine what type of pitch has been thrown (is it a curveball, a fastball, a change-up, etc.) and how fast it's coming. Second, he must determine if the pitch will be a ball (if it will pass outside the strike zone, in which case he would most likely choose not to swing the bat) or a strike (if it will pass through the strike zone, in which case he would most likely elect to swing). Third, if he does decide to swing at the

It's been said that the most difficult achievement in all of sports is to hit a major league pitch. Traveling up to 100 mph, the ball takes less than half a second from the moment it leaves the pitcher's hand to cross home plate. Indicative of the task's difficulty, the average professional baseball player generally "gets a hit" (hits the ball into fair territory and makes it safely to base) less than 3 out of 10 times at bat. A successful batter draws upon excellent hand-eye coordination, gutsy concentration, and years of diligent practice.

oncoming pitch, he must concentrate on the ball and determine where to hit it in the field.

This last decision can get quite complicated, depending on the circumstance. If it's early in the game, for example, a batter might want to play it safe by trying to hit the ball between the infielders or over their heads but short of the outfielders for a base hit (one that's good enough to safely reach base). If it's late in the game with his team trailing, the batter might go for broke, swinging the bat as hard as he can in an attempt to advance extra bases, possibly even to score a home run. There are many other scenarios that may come into play during the course of any one game. For example, the batter might have a teammate on third base in contention to score, and therefore elect to lightly tap the pitch just a few feet (called a "bunt"); by the time this surprise hit is grabbed by the opposing team, the runner on third has a good chance of sprinting to home plate to score a run.

A Statistics-Crazy Sport

To gain tactical advantage, baseball players rely more heavily on assessing opponents' past performances than players of any other sport. Every year, entire books are published containing nothing but statistical analyses of major league players. Players, coaches, managers, and avid fans all pore over these statistical tomes of player and team performances.

On the endless rows of shelves in the U.S. Library of Congress, there are more books on baseball than any other sport.

Why this seeming preoccupation with statistical analyses? There are several reasons. Each major league team plays 162 games in a regular season (April through September)—far more contests than other sports. Therefore, a careful study of each player's performance over numerous games can be extrapolated—with a fair degree of reliability—into predictive hunches about probable reactions to any number of circumstances. For example, a statistical analysis might show that Batter A is much better at hitting a curveball than a fastball, in which case the catcher will signal the pitcher to throw a fastball. By the same token, a certain Pitcher B might tend to rely on a specific pitch to save the day in a pressure situation; a smart batter will know that and be on the lookout for that predictable pitch.

Another reason for the statistical preoccupation is that baseball's tempo lends itself to circumspect decisions. In most team sports—such as basketball, soccer, and ice hockey—the action is so fast and plays occur so rapidly that there is little time for on-the-spot consideration of tactical options based upon the various players' records. In baseball, however, there is ample time between batters, between pitches, and between innings for contemplative analysis of each player's record of reactions to various situations—all this leading up to tactical decisions by coaches and managers on the sidelines and by individual players on the field. Invariably, the winning team in baseball must not only outplay but often outsmart its opponent.

Winning Strategies

At its core, baseball is a nervy contest between the pitcher and batter. A major league pitcher is a highly skilled athlete who has mastered one of sport's most difficult feats—throwing a baseball so fast, or with such deceptive speed, or with such tricky spin that an exceptionally skilled athlete, the batter, simply cannot hit the pitch or at least cannot hit it well enough to produce advantageous results.

Virtually all professional players compete on a high level both offensively and defensively, but most distinguish themselves in one specialty or the other—exceptional ability in the field or at the plate. It is somewhat uncommon to excel at both. Typically, a pitcher's playing strength is particularly lopsided—pitchers are consistently the worst batters (having batting averages often less than .200) because they concentrate almost exclusively on practicing the rarefied skills of pitching.

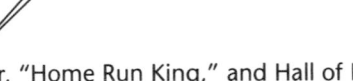

Hank Aaron, legendary major leaguer, "Home Run King," and Hall of Fame inductee, saw the contest this way: "The pitcher has got only a ball. I've got a bat. So the percentage in weapons is in my favor, and I let the fellow with the ball do the fretting."

—*Ken Burns,* Baseball: An Illustrated History

Unlike the National League, the American League excuses its pitchers from the responsibility of batting. In American League games, a "designated hitter" (called a "DH") is used whenever it becomes the pitcher's turn to bat. The DH therefore assumes the offensive role of his team's pitcher.

Like the characteristics attributed to individual players, some teams are best known for their strong hitting, others for their overpowering pitching, still others for their excellent defensive fielding. Championship teams generally demonstrate strength in each.

As a particular game progresses, it often becomes increasingly evident to the manager and coaches what their team needs to do to win. Particularly in the last few innings, a manager tends to become more active, making player substitutions to help fortify a particular strategy or to replace tired players. Unlike most team sports, once a baseball player leaves the field and is replaced by a substitute, that player cannot play again in that game.

Toward the conclusion of a game, a manager usually tries his best to avoid undue risk if his team is ahead. He will, however, push his team toward greater risks when the team is trailing with few innings remaining. For example, if his team is at bat, he might instigate more aggressive base stealing to advance players in hopes of scoring a run or multiple runs. If his team is in the field, a manager might signal his pitcher to throw four "balls" well out of the strike zone and allow the batter to go to first base (called an "intentional walk"). This would be a wise move if that batter at the plate is known for hitting home runs while the next batter in the line-up is known to be a weaker hitter with a lower batting average.

Equipment

The standard equipment for professional baseball is fairly simple. All players wear team uniforms (one style for home games, another style for away games) that consist of the following: a jersey (with each player's last name and identification number generally printed on the back), pants (with leather/elastic belt), billed caps (to shade the eyes from sunlight or bright stadium lights), stirrup socks, and flexible shoes with metal or rubber cleats (called "spikes") on the bottom for sure-footed traction. While in the field, players wear specially padded leather gloves for catching the ball (see Figure 6).

The baseball is a hard sphere measuring about nine inches in circumference. Its core is cork and rubber, around which yards and yards of wool yarn are tightly wound. The ball's cover is composed of two strips of cowhide, tightly hand-stitched together.

Because the ball is hard and pitched with such high velocity (70 to 100 mph), the batter wears a protective helmet made of plastic while at bat. For the same reasons, the catcher wears special protective gear that includes a plastic helmet, face mask, padded vest, shin guards, and a heavily padded catcher's mitt.

Though aluminum bats are permitted in collegiate baseball and are popular among the nonprofessional leagues, all bats used at the professional level must be made of wood (typically ash). Bats can be a maximum of 42 inches long.

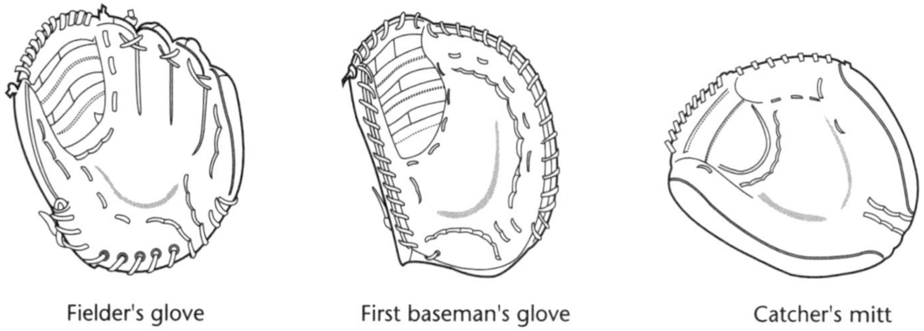

Figure 6. Players today wear various fielder's gloves—except for the first baseman and catcher, who wear specialty gloves. During the mid–nineteenth century, when baseball was in its infancy, players caught the ball bare-handed. The first gloves were introduced around 1875 but were considered unmanly by most players then. By 1895, however, all players in the field wore gloves.

Other Important Stuff

Batting average: One of the most insightful statistical evaluations of each player, it is calculated by taking the number of times the player has gotten a hit during the entire playing season and dividing it by the number of times that player has been at bat. For example, if the player has gotten 112 hits after 360 times at bat, his batting average—always taken to three decimal places—would be .311. For perspective, the typical batting average for a major league player is around .270 (in other words, he makes a hit and gets safely on base 27 percent of the time he comes to bat). A good batting average is .280 or above; very good is .300 or above.

Double play: When the offensive team has one or no outs against it, the defensive team has the potential opportunity to make a "double play," in which two outs are made during one at-bat. While very few double plays are made in a game, the most common occurs when there is one offensive player already on first base. The batter hits a weak ground ball, which is quickly caught and thrown to second before the runner from first base can get there (for a forced out), then is thrown to first base before the batter can run there. Rarer still is the triple play, in which the defensive team collects three outs during one at-bat; a triple play is one of the highest defensive achievements in baseball.

Earned run average (ERA): The average number of earned runs scored against a pitcher every nine innings. A pitcher's ERA under 4.0 is considered good; under 3.0 is very good.

Error: If, in the opinion of the official scorer, the offensive team makes a successful play because a defensive player mishandled the ball, that mistake is called an "error"; a statistical record of errors is kept for each game. In a professional baseball game, each team will usually commit less than three errors. Because teams are often closely matched, even a single error can give the opposing team the deciding advantage.

Ground rule double: If the ball is hit deep into the outfield and bounces over the fence, it is not counted as a home run. Instead, the batter is allowed to go to second base.

Infield fly: When there are two or fewer men on base and fewer than two outs and the batter hits a ball high into the air that lands in the infield or shallow outfield, the umpire will call an automatic out. (Without this rule, it would be too easy for the defensive team to make a double play.)

Lead runner: The offensive player who has progressed farthest around the bases. He is usually the defensive team's top priority to put out on any given play because he is in the best position to score a run.

No-hitter: A game in which there were no hits against the opposing pitcher, but players got on base due to walks and/or errors.

Perfect game: A very rare defensive achievement in which the pitcher for Team A pitches so well that Team B doesn't even get one player to first base. In major league baseball, a perfect game is pitched once every several years.

Runs batted in (RBI): The number of runners already on base who were able to score because of a batter's performance. Some experts consider this the best indicator of a player's batting value because it shows his ability to perform under pressure and to hit well enough to bring runners around the bases to score. A good RBI is at least 80 for an entire season; over 100 is very good.

Shutout: A game in which Team A plays defensively so well (particularly its pitcher) that no runs are scored by Team B.

History

Although baseball evolved from a long history of stick-and-ball games (particularly the English games of rounders and cricket), most experts point to a game played on June 19, 1846, in Elysian Fields, Hoboken, New Jersey, as its official genesis. On that day, a team called the New York Nine trounced (23–1) the Knickerbocker Base Ball Club, a team organized by Alexander J. Cartwright. They played by rules which Cartwright had drawn up the previous year. Although modified over the years, Cartwright's rules are considered the blueprint for the modern game of baseball.

The game's popularity was slow to spread, but by 1858 a small convention of baseball clubs had been held and a national association organized. The Civil War, however, brought about widespread appeal of the game. Soldiers often played it behind the lines and, after the war, they introduced it to their home communities.

In 1869, the Red Stockings of Cincinnati, Ohio, became the first professional team and thrashed all amateur opponents for more than a year (in their first 80 games, they won 79 and tied l). Other professional teams quickly organized, and the first professional players' league was formed in 1871. A series of rival leagues came and went, but by the end of the century the sport was dominated by the

National League, which by 1902 was grappling with growing competition from the American League.

The competitive rivalry of these two leagues, while at times bitter, has over time proven healthy for the sport. In 1903, it produced an annual challenge match between the best teams from each league. This annual match, called the World Series and held in October, pits two teams in a best-of-seven-game championship (whichever team wins four games gains victory).

In 1947, major league baseball's unspoken ban on African American players was finally broken when Branch Rickey, president of the Brooklyn Dodgers, hired infielder Jackie Robinson to play for his team.

In 1935, the general manager of the Cincinnati Reds, Larry MacPhail, introduced the first night game in major league history after erecting light towers at Crosley Field. Within six years, 11 of the 16 major league clubs had installed lights.

Today, the National League consists of 16 major league teams; the American League has 14. The teams of each league are divided into an Eastern, a Central, and a Western division. At the conclusion of each playing season (a season spans April through September, during which each team plays 162 games), the divisions within the two leagues compete in the play-offs, and the victors win what's called the "league pennant." The two pennant winners then play in the World Series.

The New York Yankees have won more consecutive World Series titles than any other team—five, from 1949 through 1953.

In addition to league and team rivalries, baseball has seen many disputes over the years between players and team owners, usually over salaries and contractual obligations. In 1994, a players' strike became so acrimonious and protracted that much of the season was lost. That year, even the World Series was canceled.

As a result of players' greater independence, arbitration, and concessions by team owners, players' salaries have skyrocketed over the past two decades. Nowadays, superstars routinely sign multiyear contracts for millions of dollars. The average annual salary for a major league player now exceeds a million dollars—compared with $450,000 in 1988 and $45,000 in 1975.

For all its contractual bellyaching, managerial tiffs, and vinegary strikes, baseball has woven itself inextricably into the fabric of American culture, mainly through the charisma and near-mythic feats of its best players—legendary heroes like Walter Johnson, Ty Cobb, Babe Ruth, Lou Gehrig, Joe DiMaggio, Ted Williams, Willie Mays, Mickey Mantle, Hank Aaron, Nolan Ryan, Roger Clemens, Mark McGwire, and many others.

The sport's popularity has also spread to other countries, notably Japan, Canada, Australia, Mexico, and other parts of Latin America.

chapter two

BASKETBALL

Basketball is a fast, action-packed game played by agile giants. The average pro stands 6 feet 7 inches tall and weighs 223 pounds. (When basketball star Wilt Chamberlain was asked how to become a great player, he quipped, "The first thing is to become seven feet tall.") Many experts agree that basketball demands more athletic skills than any other sport.

Basic Play

Two teams—each with five players—compete on a court, 94 feet by 50 feet (see Figure 7); they play both offensively and defensively. The surface of the court is polished wood, and there is a basket at each end. The baskets, attached to tempered-glass backboards, are suspended 10 feet off the floor.

The objective is to throw a ball through the opposing team's basket to score points (called "making" a basket). At the end of a game, the team with the highest score wins. Typically, each team scores about 80 to 110 points (for collegiate games, about 60 to 90 points).

A game begins with a player from each team meeting face-to-face in the midcourt circle. The referee throws the ball straight up between them, and the two players leap up and try to tap the ball to a teammate. This "jump ball" to start a game is called the "tip-off."

Each team defends one of the baskets and attempts to score points by throwing the ball through the other team's basket. The

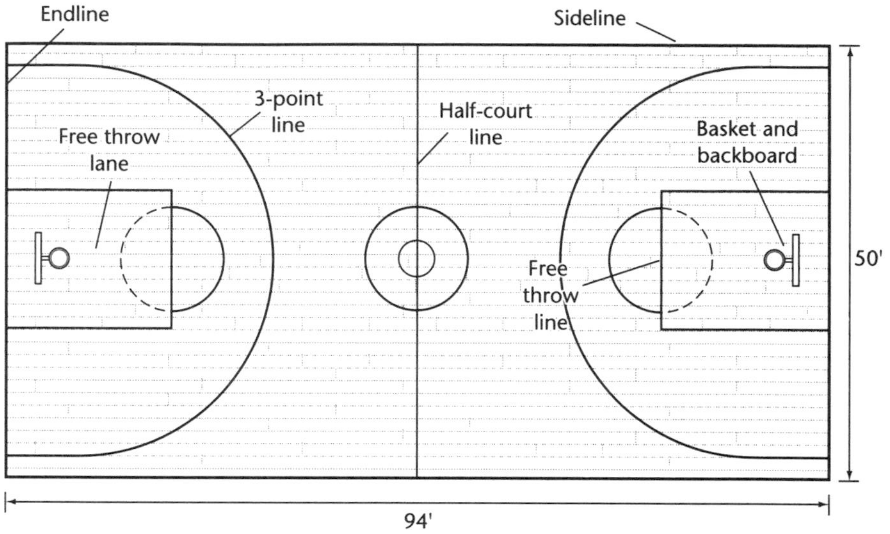

Figure 7. A basketball court has a wooden floor and measures 94 by 50 feet. At each end of the court, there is a backboard (6 by 4 feet) and basket, suspended 10 feet off the floor. At center court are two concentric circles where "jump balls" are contested. On the court in front of each basket, painted lines delineate the free throw line and lane as well as the 3-point line. In collegiate games, the 3-point arc is about four feet closer to the basket, and the free throw lane is a little more narrow.

team in control of the ball plays offense by trying to score points. The opposing team plays defense by attempting to foil offensive plays and to block shots at its basket. After a basket has been scored or after certain infractions (see "Fouls and Violations"), possession of the ball is given to the opposing team, which then plays offense.

When a shot is attempted but missed, players for both teams attempt to gain possession of the ball by grabbing the "rebound" (the ball that bounces off the metal rim of the basket or off the backboard). Because about half of all shots to the basket are unsuccessful, rebounds are very important. The team that gains possession of the ball has the opportunity to score, so the more rebounds a team captures, the more chances it has to win points.

If the offensive team captures the rebound, it will attempt to shoot again. If the ball is captured by the defensive team, it immediately becomes the offensive team and will move the ball to the other end of the court to attempt to score in its opponent's basket.

When a player is in possession of the ball, he or she has three options: (1) attempt to shoot it for a basket to score points, (2) throw it to a teammate for a tactical advantage, or (3) advance the ball by "dribbling" it (bouncing it with one hand while running or walking). A player may not hold the ball while running or walking (this is a violation called "traveling"). Once a player stops dribbling the ball, he must pass it or shoot it; he may not resume dribbling (see Figure 8).

Playing time is divided into four 12-minute quarters in professional games; there are 90-second breaks between quarters and a 15-minute break at halftime. Collegiate games are divided into two 20-minute halves with a 15-minute break. Factoring in time-outs called by the coaches (a pro team is allowed five 90-second and two 20-second

Figure 8. Of the two ways to advance the basketball, dribbling is slower than passing but is safer because the player has more control over the ball. A good dribbler is an offensive asset who can often penetrate the opposition's defense. The dribbler can also influence the pace of the game to his team's advantage.

time-outs per game; a collegiate team is permitted four 60-second and two 20-second time-outs) and suspensions in play to deal with fouls and other violations, a game normally lasts about two hours. For televised games, the number of time-outs is reduced due to commercial breaks. In case of a tie, the game continues in five-minute overtime periods until a period concludes with one team ahead on points.

"Absolute silence—that's the one thing a sportswriter can quote accurately."

—Bobby Knight, coach of Indiana University

If, during play, the ball goes out-of-bounds, an official will stop play and the clock, identify the player who touched the ball last, and award possession of the ball to the opposing team. To resume play, the official hands the ball to a player on the offensive team; that player, who stands just outside the boundary line of the court, then has five seconds to throw the ball inbounds to a teammate.

Scoring Points

Points can be scored in two ways: shooting the ball through the opponent's basket from anywhere on the court for a "field goal," or shooting a "foul shot" as compensation for having been fouled by an opponent (see "Fouls and Violations").

A field goal counts as either two or three points. If shot from within the 3-point line, the basket counts two points. If shot from outside that line, it counts three points. In professional basketball, the 3-point line is 23 feet 9 inches from the basket; in collegiate ball, it is 19 feet 9 inches away. The 3-point line was established to promote variety in shotmaking and in play action as well as to prevent the tallest players from totally dominating the game.

A foul shot counts one point; the player attempting a foul shot stands at the foul line to shoot (15 feet from the backboard). At the same time, all other players line up on each side of the free throw lane and may not interfere with the free throw attempt. If the shot is missed, the other players will attempt to grab the rebound.

In pro basketball, an average of 46 percent of 2-point shots, 37 percent of 3-point shots, and 74 percent of free throws are successful (college: 44 percent of 2-point, 34 percent of 3-point, and 67 percent of free throws).

The Players

The five players on each team may position themselves anywhere on the court. Generally, two play near the basket and are called "forwards." Another, called the "center," plays between the foul line and basket. The other two, called "guards," play to the right and left of the center a little farther out (see Figure 9). Because all top players are so highly trained, skilled, and versatile, they sometimes temporarily interchange positions and roles as the course of play requires, but their basic profiles are as follows.

Guards

Usually the shortest and quickest players, they are excellent dribblers and passers. Guards initiate most plays and direct the offense. They specialize as the "point guard" (a pro is about 6 feet 3 inches, 200 pounds, with major ballhandling responsibilities) and as the "shooting guard" (about 6 feet 6 inches, 210 pounds, and the best shooter). In women's National Collegiate Athletic Association (NCAA) basketball, guards are about 5 feet 8 inches.

Center

Usually the tallest player, best rebounder, and a good passer, he holds the pivotal position and is often the most important player. If a good shooter, too, he can dominate the game. A center is about 7 feet 2 inches tall, weighing 250 pounds. In women's NCAA basketball, she is about 6 feet 3 inches.

Forwards

Taller and stronger than guards, they play more physically, generally maneuver from free throw line to end line, and are excellent rebounders. They specialize as the "small forward" (about 6 feet 7 inches, 225 pounds, and the faster of the two forwards) and as the

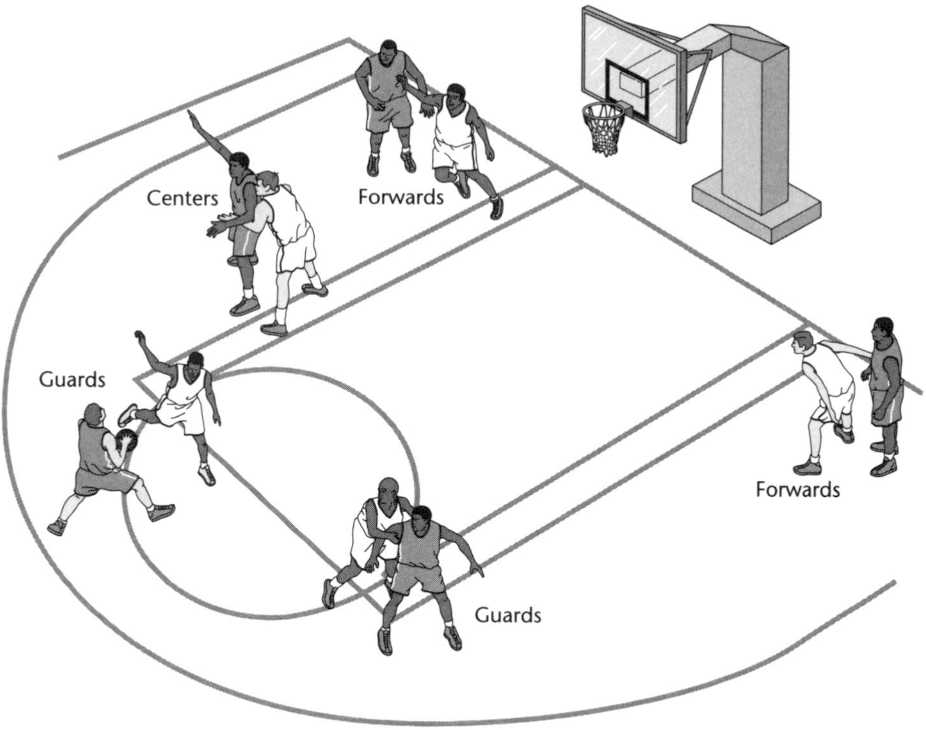

Figure 9. In general, the five players on each team play these positions: guard (two players), center (one player), and forward (two players). In this illustration, the team wearing dark uniforms is on offense (it has possession of the ball and is attempting to score). Because all professional players are highly skilled and adaptable, they often temporarily switch roles in response to fast-changing situations during a game.

"power forward" (about 6 feet 9 inches, 235 pounds, whose defensive play and aggressive rebounding complement the center). In NCAA women's play, forwards are about 6 feet.

In addition, seven other players sit on the sideline during the game and are used as substitutes for injured or tired players, for those who have fouled out of the game, or when special skills are required (for example, a specialist in making 3-point shots or a player particularly good at rebounding). Also at the sideline are the head coach (who makes these decisions and directs the team's overall strategy), two or three assistant coaches, an equipment manager, and a trainer, who is responsible for conditioning the players and for tending to injuries.

"If a coach starts listening to the fans, he winds up sitting next to them."
—Johnny Kerr, former pro basketball coach

A player's value to the team is evaluated by the average number of points he makes during a game, average number of shots he blocks, rebounds he grabs, times he steals the ball from an opponent, and "assists" he makes (an assist is a pass which directly leads to a basket being scored). A statistical record is kept on all these aspects of a player's performance throughout his career.

Fouls and Violations

There are two sets of infractions in basketball: fouls and violations. Fouls are committed against other players or the officials; violations are infractions of procedural rules.

Fouls

There are two types of fouls—personal and technical. The latter is more serious.

Except for incidental contact between players, basketball is supposed to be a noncontact sport. Therefore, penalties are assessed by the referee or umpire against a player for pushing, tripping, holding, charging, and illegal blocking. These infractions are called "personal fouls" and are common in all basketball games.

When a foul is committed, an official blows his whistle, stopping play and the game clock. He uses hand signals to inform the scorekeeper of the nature of the offense. The fouled player is permitted a free throw to the basket from the foul line and is allowed 10 seconds to attempt the shot. Each successful free throw counts one point.

If the fouled player was attempting to shoot the ball when fouled and missed the shot, he gets two free throws (if he was shooting from outside the 3-point line and missed the shot, he gets

"I only know how to play two ways: reckless and abandon."
—Magic Johnson, former star of Los Angeles Lakers

three free throws). If he was fouled but made the shot anyway, he gets one free throw.

If the player with the ball was fouled when not shooting, his team maintains possession but must take it out-of-bounds and then resume play. (In college, the ball is not taken out-of-bounds, using free throws instead. The official will award him a "one-and-one," meaning that if he makes the first foul shot he can attempt to score a second one.)

If an offensive player without the ball is fouled, play is stopped and that defensive personal foul is recorded against the offending player and his team.

If a defensive player is fouled, play is stopped and the official gives possession of the ball to the offended team.

"Technical fouls" are given to players or coaches for unsportsmanlike conduct, particularly toward an official. A technical foul gives the other team two free throws and possession of the ball.

An excessive number of offensive and defensive fouls is also punished. If a pro player commits six personal fouls (five in college), he is disqualified from playing for the rest of that game. If a player or coach commits two technical fouls, he is ejected. If, collectively, a team accrues five defensive or offensive personal fouls within a single quarter (for college, seven during a half), that team is placed in a "penalty situation," whereby the opposing team is awarded two free throws (a one-and-one in college) for every additional foul the penalty-situation team commits for the duration of that quarter (or half).

A successful coach uses the foul rules wisely and to best advantage. Toward the conclusion of a game, for example, the coach of a team behind in points might instruct his players to commit defensive personal fouls intentionally in order to stop play; then, when the offense throws the ball back into court to resume play, the defense has the chance to intercept it.

Violations

There are also penalties (called violations) for not playing by established procedures—such as illegal delays or improper ballhandling. As penalty, the offending team must relinquish possession of the ball. All penalties are tracked by the official timekeeper. Here are the rules and procedures most commonly violated:

- After being handed an out-of-bounds ball, a team has five seconds to put it back into play.
- Once in possession of the ball, the offensive team has 24 seconds (35 for men's college games, 30 for women's) to shoot it.
- Once an official has handed the ball to a team after its opponent has made a field goal, the offensive team has 10 seconds to bring the ball across the half-court line and into its opponent's territory. Once across the line, the team can't cross back. (There is no 10-second rule in women's basketball.)
- An offensive player cannot remain in the opponent's foul lane for more than three seconds at a time. (There is no time limit for defensive players.) The foul lane is also called the "key," "paint," or "3-second lane."
- Ballhandling errors, such as traveling and "double dribbling" (bouncing the ball with two hands instead of one), are also violations.

Strategies

Offense

In order to score, the team in possession of the ball will attempt to either shoot a long ball, usually a "jump shot," or, by dribbling and/or passing, maneuver through its opponent's defenses toward the basket for a close-in shot, often a "layup" or a "dunk." To make a jump shot, the ballcarrier jumps straight up and shoots the ball at the apex of his jump (see Figure 10). For a layup, the player maneuvers beneath the basket, leaps up with the ball, and makes a basket

Figure 10. The jump shot is frequently used for a 2- or 3-point and other shots away from the basket. It often enables the shooter to leap above the defender in order to release the ball uncontested.

through a glancing shot off the backboard (see Figure 11). For a dunk, the player holds the ball with one or both hands, leaps toward the basket, and with a quick, forceful motion thrusts the ball down through the hoop (see Figure 12).

To execute either tactic successfully, the offensive team relies on predetermined maneuvers (set plays that the team has practiced, such as the basic "give-and-go"—see Figure 13) or on quick, improvised maneuvers. If the intended tactic is to shoot a long 3-point ball, the team will attempt to position one of its players for an unchallenged shot at the basket. If attempting a close-in shot, the team must move the ball swiftly and deceptively to outmaneuver the opponents.

Depending on the score, on the time left to play, and on his or her assessment of the opponent's strengths and weaknesses, a coach may change his team's offensive strategy and make player substitutions several times during a game.

Figure 11. Once the offensive team has maneuvered the ball close to the opponent's basket, a player may attempt to score with a layup. This shot is usually successful; the difficulty is in penetrating the opposition's defense around the basket.

Figure 12. The dunk is another shot that is usually successful once the offense has penetrated the defense around the basket.

Defense

In pro basketball, the team whose basket is under attack plays "man-to-man" defense, meaning that each defensive player matches himself against his counterpart on the opposing team and attempts to disrupt offensive plays, block shots, and grab rebounds.

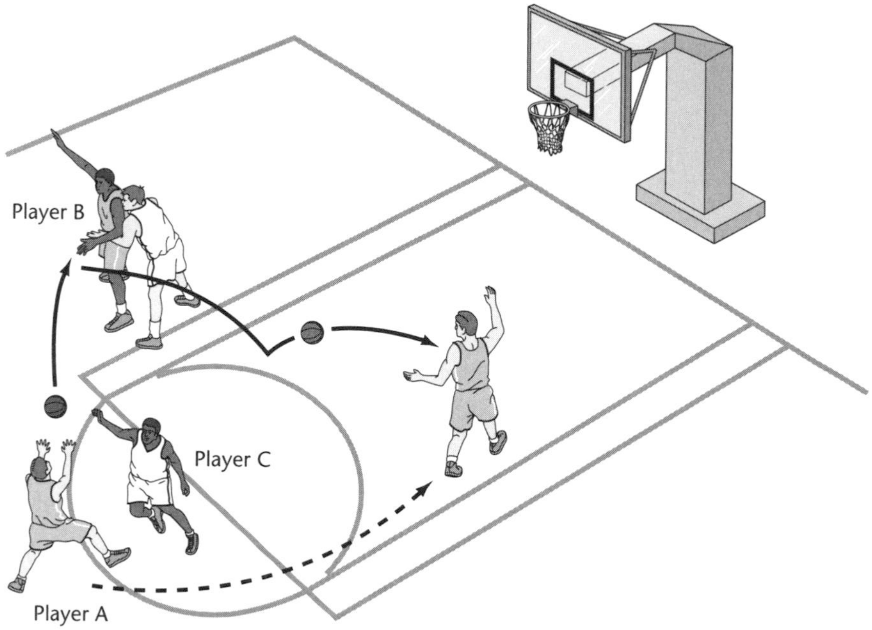

Figure 13. One of basketball's basic offensive moves, the give-and-go is designed for the player in possession of the ball (Player A) to break free of the opponent guarding him (Player C). Player A passes the ball to teammate Player B and then runs around Player C toward the basket. Player B immediately throws the ball back to Player A, now in the clear and headed for a shot at the basket.

In collegiate basketball, either man-to-man defense or the "zone" defense can be used. In the zone defense, each player is responsible for a strategic area of the court. In pro games, however, zone defenses are illegal. In 1946, the zone defense was outlawed for pro games because it tends to promote slower play and fewer shots and complements teamwork. Man-to-man defense encourages faster action and emphasizes the impressive individual talents of star athletes.

Equipment

The basketball measures nine and a half inches in diameter. It is inflated with air, and the outer cover is made of pebble-grained leather. The basket measures 18 inches across; the rim is made of metal, and the attached netting hangs down 15 to 18 inches.

A team of players wears matching sleeveless shirts and shorts, as well as high-top, lightweight leather shoes with rubber soles. The player's last name, identifying number, and team name appear on his or her shirt.

Major Competitions

At the end of the regular season (November through April, during which each team plays 82 games), the best pro teams from each of the National Basketball Association's two conferences and four divisions compete in an annual play-off series. The play-offs determine which two teams will meet for the championship, a best-of-seven-games competition (concluding in June); the first team to win four games wins the title.

"Show me a good loser, and I'll show you a loser."
—*Red Auerbach, former coach of Boston Celtics*

In collegiate basketball, the most prestigious championships are sponsored by the National Collegiate Athletic Association (NCAA). The best teams compete in a postseason tournament to determine which two teams will meet for the championship. Another significant collegiate championship is sponsored by the National Association of Intercollegiate Athletics (NAIA).

Other Important Stuff

Goaltending: If the ball has been shot toward the basket, a defensive player is allowed to attempt to block it only as it rises on its curved trajectory toward the basket. No player is allowed to tamper with the ball as it arcs downward toward the basket; that is goaltending. If goaltending is called against the defense, then the shot is counted as a score. If goaltending is committed by the offense, then the shot is not counted and the opposition is awarded possession of the ball.

Pick: A legal maneuver in which an offensive player stands still, providing a barrier (or "screen") behind which his teammate can shoot for a basket or brush past him in an attempt to break free of the defensive player guarding him.

Post: Another name for the center when playing offense.

Screen: A common play in which the player with the ball makes a maneuver so that a teammate stands between him and the defensive player. Temporarily shielded from the opposition by his teammate, the player with the ball is free to make an unchallenged shot at the basket.

Steal: When a defensive player takes the ball away from the offense either by intercepting a pass or by swatting the ball away from an opponent who is dribbling or holding it.

Turnover: Whenever possession of the ball switches to the other team because of a steal.

History

More than a century ago, basketball was created by one man. In the fall of 1891, Dr. James Naismith, a Canadian and a Presbyterian minister, was working for the International YMCA Training School (now Springfield College) in Springfield, Massachusetts. He wanted to devise a new athletic game for his students that could be played in the school's indoor gym during the winter months.

For the new game, Naismith used a soccer ball and two wooden peach baskets, which he mounted on the balcony railings at either end of the gym. (Interestingly, the peach baskets were mounted 10 feet off the floor, same as baskets today. A ladder was used to retrieve the ball from the baskets.) The first game was played in December of 1891, and the next month Naismith published in the school newspaper his 13 basic rules for the game.

The game's popularity spread to other YMCAs and to colleges; Christian missionaries exported the game to foreign countries. By the mid-1890s, several initial games had been played between collegiate teams including the University of Iowa vs. the University of Chicago, Yale vs. Pennsylvania, Stanford vs. California, and the Minnesota State School of Agriculture vs. Hamline College. The first women's collegiate basketball game was played at Smith College in 1895. The first intercollegiate league, called the Ivy League, was organized for the 1901–1902 season.

The first professional basketball league was started in 1898; it later failed but was followed by several other attempts. The National Basketball League formed in 1937, and the Basketball Association of America in 1946. These two merged in 1949 to form the National Basketball Association (NBA) with 17 teams. Today, the NBA dominates professional basketball in the United States and is composed of 29 teams. The players, who are recruited from the best collegiate teams, earn whopping salaries, averaging $2.2 million a year. Over the past three decades, the most successful pro teams have included the Boston Celtics, Los Angeles Lakers, Philadelphia 76ers, Detroit Pistons, and Chicago Bulls.

In 1996, two women's pro leagues were organized—the Women's National Basketball Association (WNBA) with 10 teams and the American Basketball League (ABL) with nine. The WNBA follows a summertime playing season while the ABL's season parallels the NBA's.

After World War II, the popularity of amateur basketball grew tremendously at the college and university level because of larger arenas, increased viewership via television, athletic scholarships, and increased revenue from paid attendance and broadcasting fees.

The National Collegiate Athletic Association (NCAA) sponsored its first basketball tournament in 1939 and today oversees about 950 men's and 960 women's basketball programs at U.S. colleges and universities. Teams from schools with the largest enrollments compete in Division I; smaller schools compete in either Division II or III. Over the past 30 years, the best men's teams in Division I have included UCLA, Duke, and North Carolina; for women, Tennessee, Stanford, Connecticut, and Louisiana Tech.

As the game attracted more and more players, it also underwent refinements. In 1893, the peach basket was replaced by a metal hoop with a net. Backboards were introduced in 1894, and a larger, specialized ball replaced the soccer ball that same year. In 1900, dribbling was permitted for men's games (previously, the ball could only be passed or shot). One-handed shots were introduced in the 1930s and the jump shot in the late 1940s. Until the late 1970s, the rules were significantly different for men's and women's games; they are now virtually identical.

chapter three

FOOTBALL

Although football trails a long tail of rules and regulations, the sport's basic premise is short and simple: get the ball across the opposition's goal line and, in the process, revel in the cuts, bumps, breaks, and bruises. The most popular spectator sport in America, football is a compelling combination of brute force and nimble feet—all played to the multidecibel din of huge stadium crowds.

With 22 immensely strong, highly charged players clashing in this contact sport, numerous rules and seven on-field officials are employed to prevent competitions from becoming gladiatorial contests.

The Basics

The game is played by two teams—each with 11 players—on a large playing field of grass or artificial turf measuring 100 yards long by 53 yards wide (see Figure 14). The field is marked off with white lines (called "yard lines") running crosswise every five yards to chart a team's progress toward its opponent's goal line. (Yard lines are numbered on the field in ascending increments of 10 to the 50-yard line in the middle of the field, then in descending order to the opposing goal line.) At each end of the field are a goal line and a goalpost consisting of two upright posts and a crossbar.

Play begins with a "kickoff." It's preceded by a coin toss to determine which team will kick and which will receive, as well as which

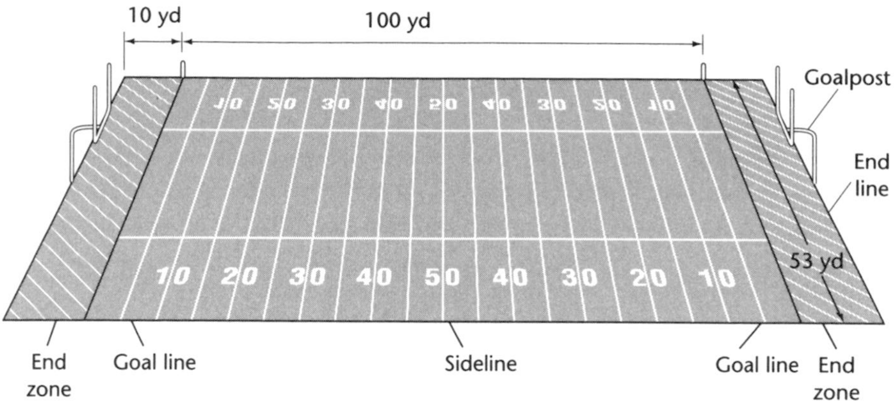

Figure 14. A football field is 53 yards wide and—from goal line to goal line—100 yards long. At each end is an end zone, measuring 10 yards from goal line to end line. At each end line is a goalpost, consisting of two uprights and a crossbar. The field is marked every five yards by white "yard lines" running crosswise.

goal line each team will defend. Standing at least 10 yards apart, the two teams line up across the field, facing each other with their backs to their respective goal lines. One team presents the ball to the opposition by kicking it downfield from its own 30-yard line (35 for college). Once a member of the opposing team catches the football, his team tries to move the ball toward the opponent's goal line to score points—usually through a succession of attempts called "plays."

Except for kickoffs, each play begins at an imaginary line crosswise to the field called the "line of scrimmage" (or "the line"), which is the demarcation between offense and defense and is reestablished at the end of each play (where a ballcarrier is tackled or run out of bounds). To get set for the next play, the defensive players line up on one side of the line, offensive players on the other. Neither is allowed across until the ball is snapped.

The ultimate object of the game is for a player on the team with the football (the offensive team, which has "possession" of the ball) to either run with it across the opponent's goal line for a six-point "touchdown" or to throw the ball (called a "pass") to a teammate who is already across the goal line and catches it (also a six-point touchdown). In certain situations, the team in possession of the ball can also score one or three points by kicking the ball over the goal-post's crossbar and between the uprights (more on that later).

Meanwhile, the team playing defense makes every effort to thwart the offensive team's attempts to score by tackling the runner with the ball, by swatting down or intercepting passes, or by blocking kicks.

"Football is two things: blocking and tackling."
—*Vince Lombardi, Green Bay Packers coach, 1959–1968*

This offense-vs.-defense battle rages up and down the playing field through a series of skirmishes called plays. A play is initiated when the center hands the ball ("snaps" the ball) to the quarterback; a play ends when an official blows his whistle and declares the ball "dead" (a ball is called dead if the ballcarrier is tackled or runs out of bounds, if the quarterback throws an incomplete pass, or if a team scores).

The offensive team is permitted to retain possession of the ball—and to maintain its drive to score a touchdown—so long as it moves the ball, either by running with it or throwing it to a teammate, at least 10 yards closer to the opponent's goal line in four plays or fewer (each play represents one "down"). If the offensive team gains at least 10 yards in four downs or fewer, then it is rewarded with another set of four downs to cover another 10 yards—and so forth as it progresses across the opponent's goal line for a touchdown. If, however, the team fails to gain 10 yards in four downs, it must relinquish possession of the ball to the opposition, which then begins its drive to score in the opposite direction. Here are two examples:

1. Team A kicks off to Team B. A player for Team B catches the ball on his 10-yard line and runs forward until he's tackled on his 45-yard line. At that point, Team B begins its four downs to gain at least 10

"I never tried to keep football simple. If your offense is simple, it's simple to stop. If your defense is simple, it's simple to attack."
—John Madden, TV commentator and former NFL coach

yards—or else must relinquish possession of the football to Team A. With the ball at the 45-yard line, the referee announces that Team B is "first and 10" (meaning that Team B is beginning its first down with 10 yards to go). On the next play, a short pass is caught by a Team B receiver before being tackled for a gain of seven yards, putting Team B across the 50-yard line and on Team A's 48-yard line. The referee announces that Team B is now "second and three" (second down with three yards to go before earning a new set of four downs). On the next play, a player for Team B runs with the ball to the 44-yard line before being tackled and makes the first down. Team B now has four more plays in which to gain another 10 yards.

2. Team A's quarterback throws a pass that is intercepted by a player for Team B, who is tackled on the 50-yard line. To start the next play, Team B is "first and 10." It will be rewarded a new first down if—within four plays—it can move the ball at least to the 40-yard line in the opponent's half of the field.

If, after its third down, the offensive team predicts that on the next play it is highly unlikely to gain enough yardage to earn a first down, the team will usually elect to kick ("punt") the ball far downfield to its opponents—rather than permit the opposing team to take possession wherever the ballcarrier is tackled on the fourth-down play. At least by punting the ball, the team forces the opposition to take possession a greater distance from its goal line.

To punt the ball, a special kicker replaces the quarterback and stands about 10 yards behind the center to receive the snap. Upon receiving the ball, he kicks it high and far (a good punt travels about 45 yards past the line of scrimmage), which gives his teammates time to run downfield to tackle the receiver.

As an alternative to punting the ball on fourth down, the offensive team can attempt to kick a "field goal" to score three points (see "Field Goal").

If the offensive team is behind in the score with little time left in the game, it will usually take the fourth-down gamble of attempting to gain sufficient yardage for a first down either by running or passing the ball. Gaining the first down is the only way for the team to retain possession of the ball and maintain some chance of scoring a touchdown.

A statistical evaluation of a team's overall performance usually factors in the number of first downs it has achieved (also calculated by its "third-down efficiency"). In addition to the number of games a team wins, loses, and ties, other frequently weighed factors include the team's number of turnovers (fumbles and interceptions), total yardage lost to penalties, total number of yards gained on offense, total number of yards allowed on defense, and total time of possession (a measure of dominance and control of the game).

Scoring Points

In addition to scoring six points for a touchdown, there are three other methods of gaining points.

Extra Point(s)

Immediately after each touchdown, the scoring team is permitted a bonus play; it can choose to attempt a one- or a two-point play. Either way, the offensive team (that just scored a touchdown) begins the bonus play at its opponent's two-yard line (three-yard line in college).

To try the one-point play, the center snaps the ball to a teammate standing seven yards behind him. Assisting in what's called a "place-kick," that player holds the ball at ground level, tilted upward, for the kicker to boot over the goalpost's crossbar. If the ball sails over the crossbar and between the uprights, the team receives one extra point, totaling seven points including the six-point touchdown. Pro teams successfully kick the extra point about 95 percent of the time. (Note: An extra-point kick travels at least 19 yards; kicked from the nine-yard line, the football must clear the crossbar at the end line, which is 10 yards behind the goal line.)

To attempt the two-point play, the offense initiates play from the same yard line but must score a "touchdown" by either running or passing the ball over the goal line. On average, pro teams are 48 percent successful at this optional play, called a "two-point conversion." Although riskier than kicking the extra point, the two-point conversion earns the team a total of eight points including the six-point touchdown. This chancier option is often taken in the final minutes of a close-scoring game, where one more point could make the winning—or at least tying—difference.

After the team attempts either the extra-point or two-point-conversion play, it then kicks off to the opposition.

Field Goal

The offensive team, at its discretion, may attempt a three-point "field goal" instead of driving for a first down or punting. Like an extra-point kick, a holder positions the football, and the kicker tries to boot it over the goalpost's crossbar.

Field goals are usually attempted when a team is both (1) on fourth down and doubts it can attain a first down and (2) is "within field goal range"—generally when the line of scrimmage is at least at the opponent's 35-yard line (which would require the football to be kicked at least 52 yards, that is, 10 + 35 + 7). If the field goal is successful, then that team kicks off to the opposition. If the attempt fails, then the opposition takes possession where the ball was kicked (if that would put the ball within the 20-yard line, then the team taking possession instead begins its offensive drive at its 20-yard line).

Safety

If the defensive team tackles the ballcarrier within the offensive team's own end zone, it's called a "safety." Not only is the defense awarded two points, but immediately it receives possession of the ball via a kick or punt from the opponent's 20-yard line. A safety is not called if a player catches a kicked ball or intercepts a pass in his own end zone and is tackled there. In those two cases, a "touchback" is declared, and the team which caught the ball begins its possession on its own 20-yard line.

Time Factors

A game is divided into four 15-minute periods called "quarters"—these are grouped into a "first half" and a "second half," separated by a 12-minute intermission called "halftime." The game clock on the scoreboard counts down (in minutes and seconds) by quarter, and is stopped by the official when the ball goes out-of-bounds, when a score is made, for an incomplete pass, a foul, a change of possession, or when a time-out is called. At the conclusion of the first, second, and third quarters, the teams switch goals. Therefore, the ball is placed on the corresponding yard line on the opposite side of the 50-yard line. A two-minute break is declared for this to take place.

During each half, a team is permitted to call three 1-minute, 50-second time-outs (except during the final two minutes of each half, when a time-out lasts only 30 seconds). In college, a time-out lasts a minute.

If a pro game is tied at the end of regulation play, a three-minute intermission is called. Then, after a coin toss to decide who kicks off to whom, the game shifts into a 15-minute, "sudden-death" overtime period—during which the first team to score wins the game. Each team is allowed two time-outs during an overtime period. If still tied after the overtime period, the game is declared a tie—unless it is a play-off game, in which case subsequent overtimes are held until one team scores.

Most collegiate teams resort to a different overtime procedure to break a tie. Each team is given the ball at its opponent's 25-yard line and attempts to score by conventional methods. Possession alternates until a victor emerges.

There is also a limit on the time permitted between plays. The offensive team is given 40 seconds to initiate play after each down. (Failure to do so means a five-yard penalty.) Collegiate teams have 25 seconds to initiate a play from the time an official sets the ball on the ground for play after the down.

The Players Are Key

The key to understanding football is to understand the function of each player on the field (see Figure 15). Like the various pieces on a giant, animated chessboard, each player has a specific role in the game's dynamics and in his team's offensive or defensive strategies.

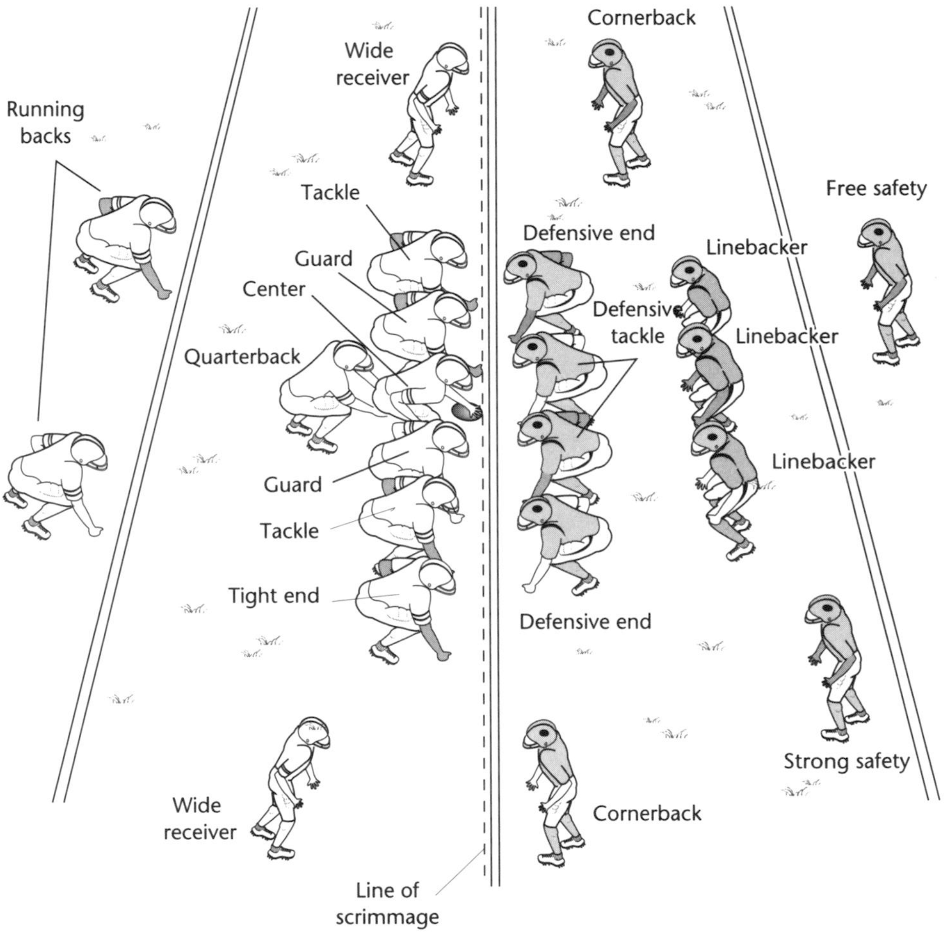

Figure 15. There are 11 offensive and 11 defensive player positions. Throughout a game, teams choose from a variety of formations in order to execute a broad range of offensive and defensive strategies. In this example, the offensive team is in a "pro set" formation; the defensive team has chosen a "4-3 defense."

Between plays, a coach can substitute one player for another and can make as many substitutions during the course of a game as he wants.

Unique among team sports, each football team has two full sets of players—one designated to play offense by attempting to score points, the other to play defense by attempting to prevent the opposition from scoring.

Regarding the following profiles for offensive and defensive players, note that pros are about 5 to 10 percent heavier than their counterparts on top-ranked collegiate teams.

The Eleven Offensive Players

The principal skills of offensive players are blocking, passing, catching ("receiving"), and running. Exactly seven offensive players must line up on the line of scrimmage; the other four must play at least a yard back. The quarterback is the offensive team's pivotal playmaker, who—after receiving the ball on the snap from the center—usually either passes the ball to one of the two wide receivers or the tight end, or hands it off to one of the two running backs for a running play. Meanwhile, it's the job of the offensive linemen (the center, two guards, and two tackles) to block and prevent the onrushing defensive players from tackling the quarterback before he can throw the ball, or to knock aside the defensive players so that a running back with the ball can dash through the defensive line for a valuable gain in yardage.

Quarterback (about 6' 3", 215 lb.): Often the star of the team, he is an exceptional athlete, a quick thinker, and an innovative playmaker who must maintain his composure under extreme pressure. He is an excellent passer (about 58 percent of his passes are caught by the intended receiver) and good at deceptive moves in the backfield to confuse or outwit the onrushing defensive players. Using codes to save time, he tells teammates what to do for each play during brief between-play meetings called "huddles." In pro games, he is permitted to receive instructions from the coach (on the sideline) via a small one-way radio mounted in his helmet. (Abbreviated QB)

Running backs (about 6' 0", 215 lb.): These are the two versatile players in the offensive backfield with the quarterback. The quarterback often hands the football to a running back for running plays and sometimes passes the ball to a running back for short-yardage plays. One of the running backs is called a *fullback* (about 240 lb.)—he's bigger and stronger to carry the ball short distances, to provide extra blocking protection for the quarterback on a passing play, or to provide blocking for the other running back, who more often is given the ball. This other running back, called the *halfback* (about 200 lb.), is lighter and faster and is often given the ball for running plays and sometimes catches short-yardage passes. Running backs make a significant number of all touchdowns. (Abbreviated RB, FB, HB)

Wide receivers or **wideouts** (about 6' 1", 200 lb.): Usually one on each extreme end of the offensive line, they are excellent athletes, very fast runners, and excellent pass receivers. As both race downfield to catch a pass from the quarterback for moderate to long yardage gains, these high-profile players gain glory by making spectacular catches and for making more touchdowns than any other players. Capable of great bursts of speed, they can run 40 yards in just a hair over four seconds. (Abbreviated WR)

Tight end (about 6' 2", 250 lb.): A strong, versatile player positioned on the left or right side of the offensive line to block onrushing defenders and sometimes to run downfield to catch a pass from the quarterback. Whichever side of the line he's positioned on is called the "strong side." (Abbreviated TE)

Linemen: These are the only players ineligible to receive a pass.

- *Center* (about 6' 4", 300 lb.): The center occupies a key position in the middle of the offensive line. To initiate a play, he's responsible for snapping the ball through his legs to the quarterback, who stands directly behind him or, on some plays, about five yards back. After the snap, the center immediately engages onrushing defenders by blocking. (Abbreviated C)
- *Guards* (about 6' 3", 305 lb.): These two linemen are responsible either for blocking onrushing defenders to prevent them from tackling the quarterback on passing plays or for knocking defenders aside to open holes in the defensive line through which a ballcarrier (usually a running back) can dash. (Abbreviated G)
- *Offensive tackles* (about 6' 6", 310 lb.): The biggest, strongest players on offense are the offensive tackles, and like the

guards, they block onrushing defenders on passing plays and attempt to bash holes in the defensive line on running plays. (Abbreviated T or OT)

Kicker (about 6' 0", 190 lb.): A kicker is used only for plays involving kickoffs, extra-point, and field-goal attempts. (Abbreviated K)

Punter (about 6' 3", 210 lb.): Used only for plays involving punting (usually fourth downs), the punter takes the place of the quarterback on those plays. (Abbreviated P)

The Eleven Defensive Players

The principal skills of defensive players are tackling and pass coverage. Unlike the offensive team, the defensive team is permitted as many or as few players on the line of scrimmage as it chooses. A typical formation positions four defensive linemen (two tackles and two ends) on the line of scrimmage whose job is to crash through the offensive line and to tackle whichever player has the ball (the quarterback or a running back). Positioned behind the defensive linemen, three linebackers either rush forward with the linemen or hang back to defend against a running play or a short pass play. To guard against and break up a passing play, two cornerbacks closely shadow the offense's wide receivers as they race downfield for a pass. In the backfield, the two safeties are the last line of defense either against a ball-carrying runner who has broken through the primary defenses or against a long pass to a fast-running wide receiver.

Defensive tackles (about 6' 3", 300 lb.): Big, but not quite as big as their offensive counterparts, defensive tackles must be big and quick to charge across the line of scrimmage and tackle whoever has the ball, and strong enough to clash with offensive guards and tackles. (Abbreviated DT)

Defensive ends (about 6' 5", 280 lb.): Essentially, defensive ends serve the same role as defensive tackles. (Abbreviated DE)

Nose tackle (about 6' 3", 320 lb.): Sometimes, the defense will use just three linemen instead of four. In those situations, a nose tackle—usually the heaviest, strongest man on the field—will position himself between the two defensive ends and opposite the center. (Abbreviated NT)

Linebackers (about 6' 3", 245 lb.): Three or four linebackers are positioned a few yards behind the linemen either to tackle an offensive ballcarrier (usually a running back) who has broken through the barrier of defensive linemen or to break up short-yardage passing plays (to a tight end, running back, or wide receiver). (Abbreviated LB)

Defensive backs (Abbreviated DB):

- *Cornerbacks* (about 5' 11", 190 lb.): Usually two, they position themselves a couple of yards behind the line of scrimmage and directly across from the men they cover, the wide receivers. Like wide receivers, cornerbacks are quick and nimble. They must also be good jumpers to bat down or intercept passes intended for wide receivers. (Abbreviated CB)
- *Strong safety* (about 6' 0", 210 lb.): He is fast and agile, with primary responsibility to cover the tight end when he sprints downfield on a passing play. He also backs up linebackers on a running play if a ball-carrying running back manages to break free of the linemen and linebackers. (Abbreviated SS or S)
- *Free safety* (about 6' 0", 205 lb.): Roaming the backfield, backing up the team, and providing the final defensive barrier, the free safety must be fast enough to cover a fleet-footed wide receiver who has outdistanced a cornerback, and strong enough to tackle a running back who has broken through all other defenses and is headed for a touchdown. (Abbreviated FS or S)

Strategies and Formations

Football teams rely on strategy, power, skill, and deception to win games. Some teams favor a passing game, others a running game. All teams incorporate a mix of both into their strategic plans, always mindful of their own players' strengths and weaknesses as well as those of the opposition. As a game progresses, strategies often change, sometimes radically. Such decisions are up to each team's head coach and his advisory staff on the sideline. They usually take the following factors into consideration: the down and yardage needed for a first down, field position (how close to the goal line), the score, and time remaining in the game.

Running plays are less risky but on average gain only 3.8 yards per play. Passing plays, on the other hand, average 11.6 yards per completion, but are successful just 58 percent of the time. The biggest drawback to the passing play is the significant risk that the ball will be caught ("intercepted") by an opposing player; an interception causes loss of possession for the team that threw the ball. Another drawback to the pass is an "incomplete" (a pass that no one catches), which provides no gain in yardage but causes the loss of a down.

Late in a game, passing plays can make more sense for the team on offense that's losing—not only because of a pass's potential for greater yardage but also because passing can conserve time on the game clock (the clock stops when a receiver runs out of bounds or when a pass is incomplete).

"If I ever need a brain transplant, I want one from a sportswriter, because I'll know it's never been used."

—Joe Paterno, Penn State football coach

To get set for the various plays, offensive players arrange themselves in tactical formations at the line of scrimmage. Judging from the offense's formation, the defensive players will arrange themselves to best counter whatever they guess is the plan of action. Once the offensive players have taken their positions, they must remain stationary until the center snaps the ball—except for one player in the backfield, called "man in motion," who is allowed to run parallel to or away from the line of scrimmage before the ball is snapped. The defensive players, however, are permitted to change positions before the ball in snapped.

The following are frequently used offensive formations, as well as the likely defensive formations used as countermeasures.

Pro Set Versus 4-3 Defense

The "pro set" offensive formation gives the quarterback the option of implementing a running or a passing play. With two running backs (the fullback is larger; the halfback is faster) at his flanks, the quarterback can easily turn and hand off the ball to one of them for a running play. Or, with two wide receivers and the tight end as pass receivers, he can throw the ball to one of them (see Figure 15).

To counteract a pro set, the opposition might form a "4-3 defense"—meaning four linemen (two ends, two tackles) and three linebackers. In the next illustration (see Figure 16), one linebacker (an outside linebacker, OLB) is positioned on the line of scrimmage to exert added pressure on the quarterback, but it's still called a "4-3 defense" (the numbers always refer only to the number of linemen and linebackers). Two other linebackers (a middle linebacker, MLB, and another outside linebacker) hang back a couple of yards, poised to join the rush if it becomes a running play or to cover and tackle receivers in the event of a passing play. The two cornerbacks cover the two wide receivers, and the two safeties provide the last line of defense.

Shotgun Versus Nickel Defense

The "shotgun" formation is geared for a passing play. In addition to the tight end, it employs three wide receivers as possible pass receivers instead of the usual two. A halfback is positioned slightly ahead of the quarterback to block onrushing defenders. To receive the snap, the quarterback positions himself about five yards behind the center to give himself more time to scan the field, pick out a receiver, and throw the ball (see Figure 17).

As a countermeasure, the defensive team might employ the "nickel defense," meaning that a fifth defensive back (usually a third cornerback who replaces one linebacker) joins two cornerbacks and two safeties. This gives the defense more coverage against the offense's extra receivers. (In some cases, the defense will use a "dime defense," in which two extra defensive backs replace two linebackers. While this provides extra-heavy protection against a passing play, it also opens up an opportunity for the offense to execute a short-yardage running play.)

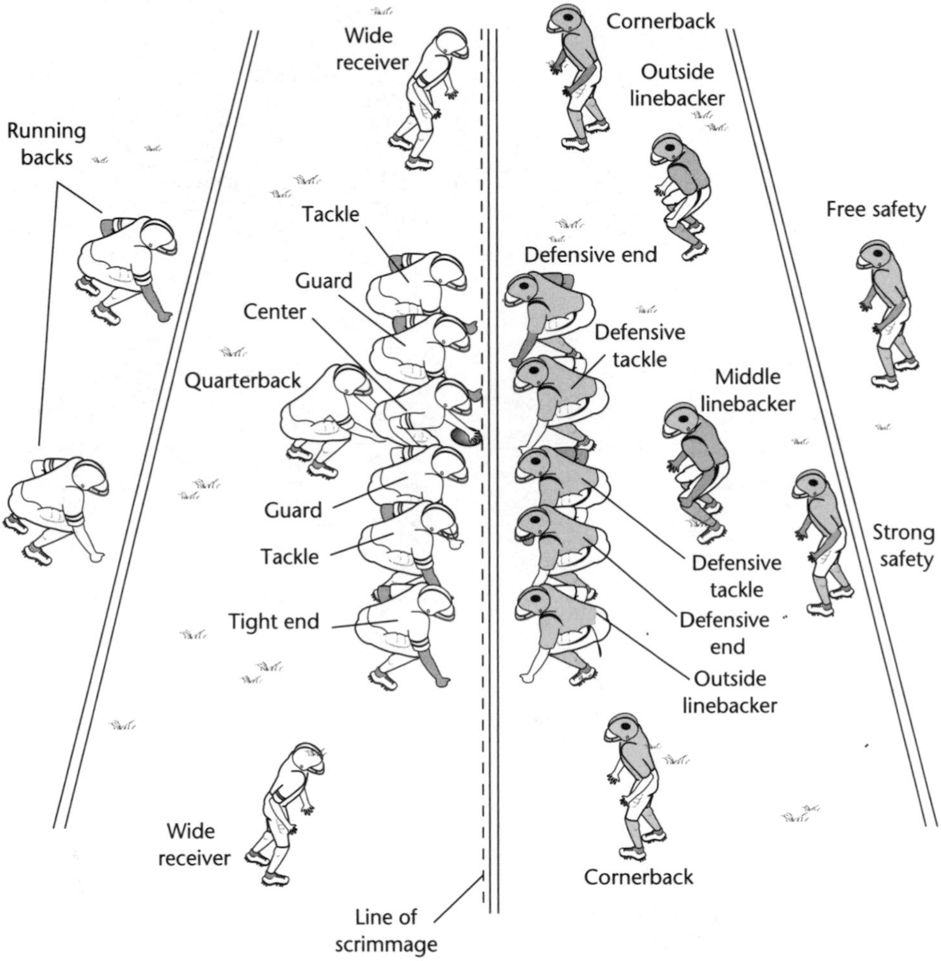

Figure 16. The pro set is a well-balanced offensive formation that facilitates either a running or a passing play. As a countermeasure, the opposing team might form a 4-3 defense (four linemen and three linebackers). The linebackers are poised to guard against a run or, in the event of a pass, to drop back to assist the two cornerbacks and safeties.

Short Yardage Versus Goal Line Defense

A "short yardage" offensive formation provides extra power for a running play, designed to ram directly into the defensive line and create a small breach for a short-yardage gain (usually less than three yards). It's used in tense situations where the offense needs to muscle the ball just a few feet forward in order to score a touchdown or

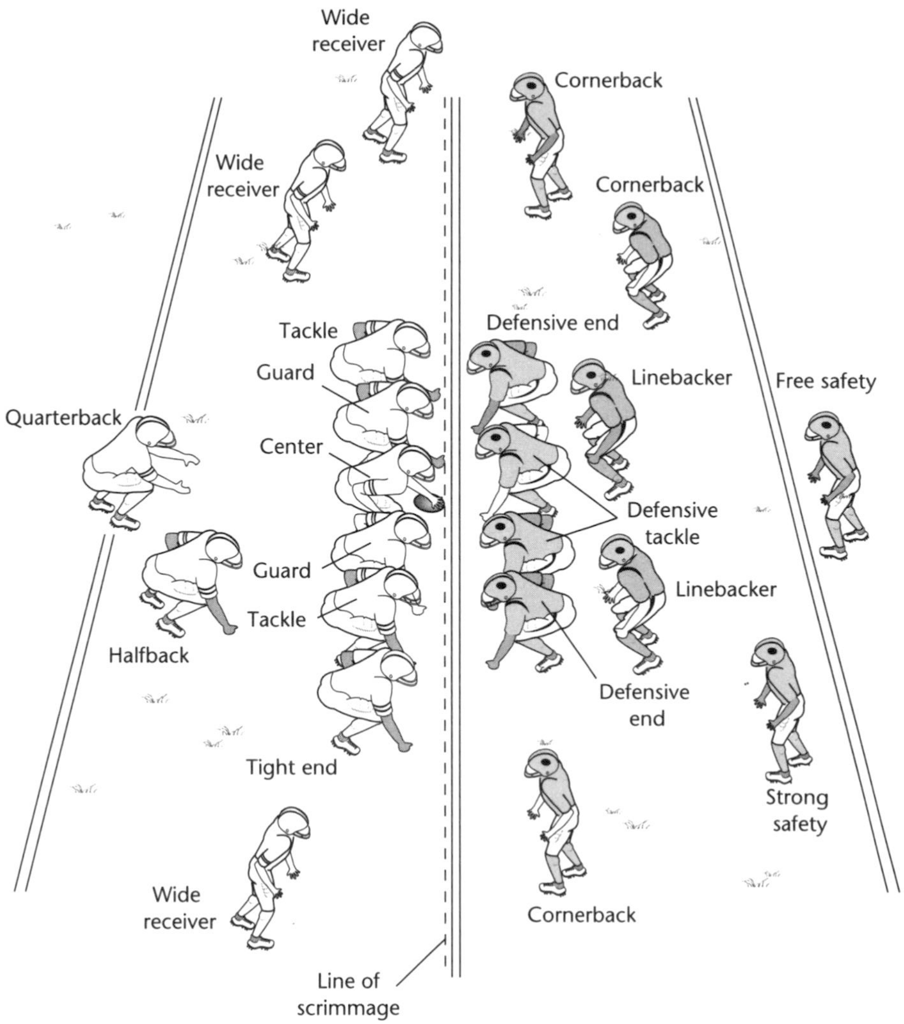

Figure 17. The shotgun offensive formation is geared for a passing play. Four receivers (instead of the typical three) race downfield to catch the quarterback's pass. The opposing team might form the nickel defense, which places a fifth man in the backfield to help thwart a passing play.

to gain a particularly important first down. Note that there are three tight ends (sometimes two with one wide receiver) packed in closely to provide concentrated blocking. In this formation, where the two running backs line up directly behind the quarterback in a so-called "I formation," the larger fullback blocks for the halfback (called the tailback, TB, in this formation), who is usually handed the football by the quarterback to run straight through the fray at the line of scrimmage (see Figure 18).

As a countermeasure, the defensive team will usually form a "goal line defense," crowding players close to the line of scrimmage to repel the offensive surge and placing one linebacker and the two

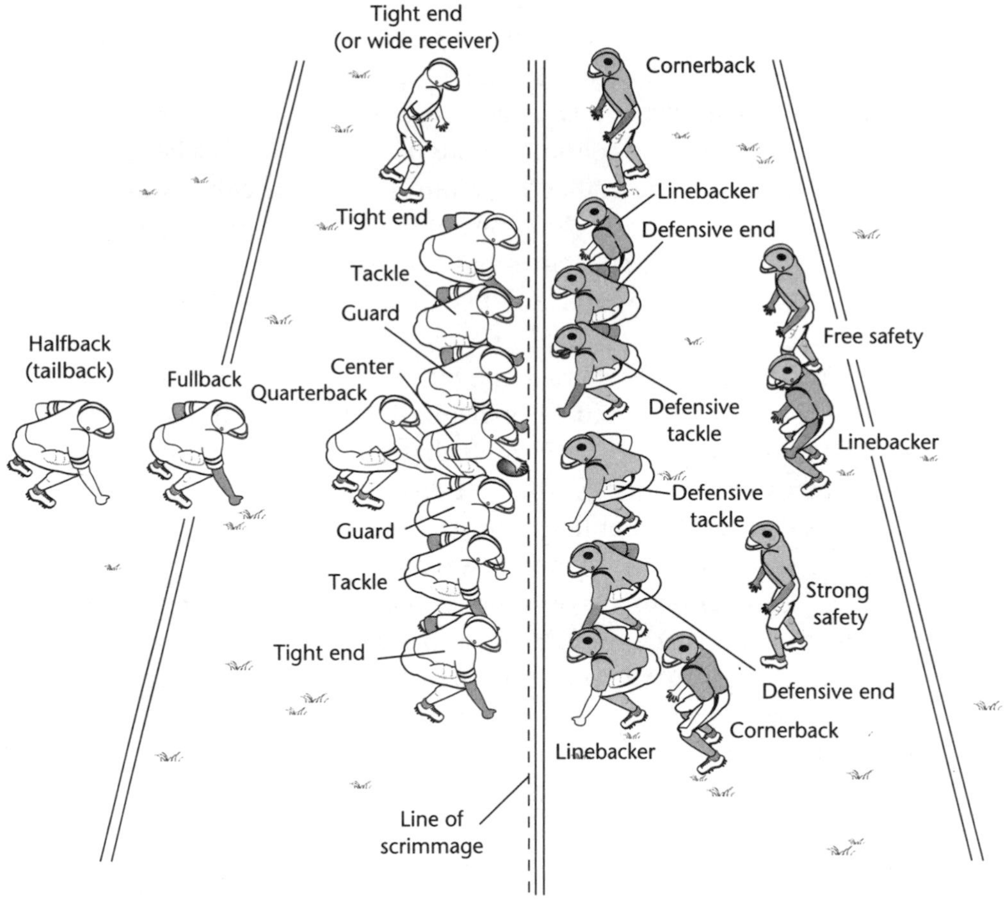

Figure 18. A short yardage offensive formation provides concentrated muscle at the line of scrimmage to ram forward just a few feet to gain a touchdown or critical first down. Most offensive players bunch close to the center to batter the defensive line, and the quarterback usually gives the ball to the halfback, who runs straight up the middle. As a countermeasure, the opposing team often forms a goal line defense, concentrating most of its players at the line to repel the brute-force attack.

safeties just behind the linemen for extra fortification and to protect against the possibility of a surprise short pass.

Alive and Kicking

Depending on the type of kick and situation, the kicked ball is governed by varying rules.

On a kickoff, possession of the football automatically ends once the ball has traveled 10 yards. After that, it becomes a "loose ball"—either team can gain possession of it by grabbing and holding on to it first. Usually, a member of the receiving team catches it, establishing possession. If the kickoff goes out-of-bounds before a player touches it, the receiving team has the choice of taking possession either where it crossed the sideline or at its own 40-yard line (35-yard line in college).

On a punt, possession automatically shifts to the receiving team. A member of the receiving team can choose to (1) catch the ball and run with it, (2) raise one hand to signal a "fair catch," which downs the ball where he catches it without fear of being tackled, or (3) let the ball hit the ground and bounce until it stops rolling—at which point that team's first-down play begins. If the ball bounces out-of-bounds, the first down begins where it crossed over the sideline. If it bounces into the receiving team's end zone, the ball is placed on that team's 20-yard line to begin its first-down play. If a receiving-team player touches the punted ball but does not catch it, the ball is declared "live" and can be recovered by either team. If a player for the punting team touches the ball first, that place is where the ball is down and where the receiving team begins its first-down play.

On a field-goal attempt, the ball is immediately declared dead after an official determines if the attempt was successful or not. A kickoff follows.

Fouls and Penalties

There are more than 100 types of fouls in football that can be committed by offensive and defensive players. Some are procedural infractions and carry modest punishment. Other transgressions, called personal fouls, are more serious because they present the danger of bodily harm; these carry heavier penalties. A foul is indicated when an on-field official throws a bright gold flag to the ground. Once the play is over, the officials levy the appropriate penalty and, using arm and hand signals, communicate the nature of the foul to the spectators.

Penalties usually involve a loss of yardage (and sometimes of a down) against the team that committed the foul. If it's an offensive foul, the official moves the ball a certain number of yards—usually 5, 10, or 15 yards from the previous play's line of scrimmage—farther away from the defense's goal line. If a defensive foul, the ball is moved closer to the defense's goal line.

The team which did not commit the foul is given the option of accepting or declining the penalty. If accepted, the penalty is enacted and the down is usually replayed. If the penalty is declined, the yardage gained or lost on the play stays intact and the down is counted as if the foul never occurred. In some situations, the team against which the foul was committed is better off to decline the penalty (for example, the team on offense will decline a defensive penalty on a play in which it gained substantial yardage despite the defensive foul).

Common procedural fouls—each punished by a five-yard penalty—include "delay of game" (that is, not beginning the next play within 40 seconds) and "offsides"/"encroachment"/"false start" (a player on the line of scrimmage moves illegally before the ball is snapped). More serious fouls include "illegal blocking," "clipping" (blocking an opponent from behind and below the waist), "facemask" (grabbing another player's), and "unnecessary roughness"—any of which is punished by a 15-yard penalty and an automatic first down. "Pass interference" is usually called when a defensive player significantly interferes with the intended receiver's effort to catch a pass. The penalty is an automatic first down for the offensive team where the foul was committed. (In college, pass interference results in a 5- or 10-yard penalty taken from the line of scrimmage, plus an automatic first down.)

Equipment

The football is a 15-ounce, pressure-inflated ball with a pebble-grain leather cover and distinctive white laces. Oval-shaped, it is 11 inches long and 21 inches around the middle (see Figure 19).

Figure 19. The football is akin to its precursor, the rugby ball. Its distinctive laces accommodate the quarterback's grip when throwing it, and its oval shape aids its flight when thrown.

To protect himself from serious injury, each player is clad in gladiatorial "armor" including shock-resistant, polycarbonate-alloy helmets with face guard and chin strap, a protective mouthpiece, and lots of reinforced padding (made of hard plastic, vinyl, and open-cell foam) for the neck, shoulders, chest, hips, tailbone, thighs, knees, and elbows. A uniform is worn over the padding, and the player's last name and identifying number are printed on his jersey. Tape is wrapped around ankles, wrists, and knees to prevent sprains and dislocations. Shoes have half-inch rubber cleats for playing on grass. For artificial turf, tennis/basketball shoes are usually worn (see Figure 20).

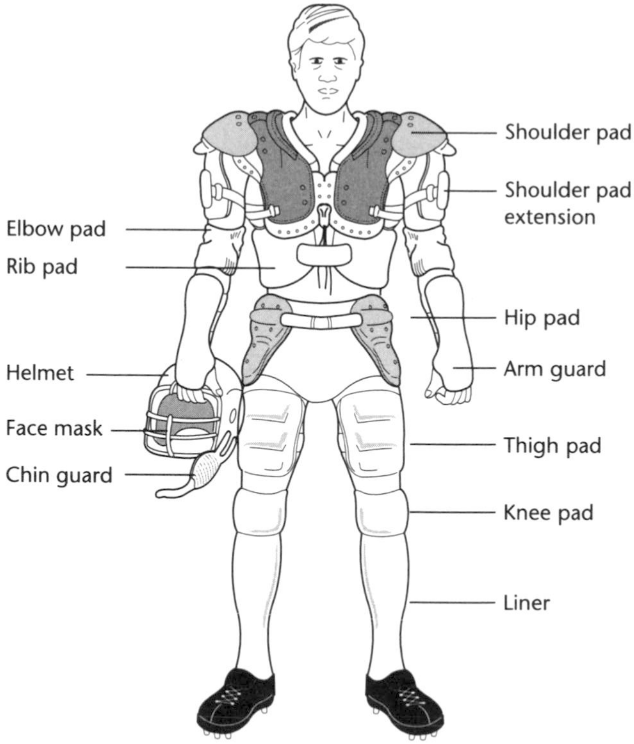

Figure 20. Resembling a gladiator clad for combat, a football player wears about 15 pounds of "armor." The padding is designed to protect the player from bone-crushing impact without significantly impeding movement.

The entire uniform weighs about 15 pounds and costs approximately $500.

Other Important Stuff

Blitz: An aggressive defensive play in which linebackers and/or defensive backs join the linemen in charging across the line to tackle the quarterback or other ballcarrier.

Bomb: Any long pass (typically 30 or more yards), usually thrown by the quarterback to a wide receiver.

Chain crew: A three-man team of officials just off the field at the sideline who keep track of the number of downs and of how many yards the offensive team needs to gain a new first down. The "rodmen" carry two poles connected by a 10-yard length of chain and, on request, measure from the point of the ball's position on the field at first down to its current position. If any portion of the ball is beyond the measuring pole, the offensive team gains a new first down. The third crewman holds another pole called the "down marker"; it shows what down is to be played next.

Draw: A deceptive play in which the quarterback takes the snap from the center, steps back a few paces as if preparing to throw the ball, but instead hands it to a running back for a surprise running play.

Fumble: If the ballcarrier drops the football, it becomes a "live" ball and can be recovered by either team. If he drops the ball while attempting to catch a pass, however, it is considered an incomplete pass with no loss of possession. If he loses the ball after he hits the ground, the ball is "dead" so there is no fumble.

"Hail Mary": An extremely long pass thrown in desperation, usually by the quarterback. The offense can only hope and pray that one of the wide receivers will catch it.

Man-to-man defense: Each linebacker and defensive back is assigned a particular offensive player to cover against a pass. Linebackers usually cover running backs; cornerbacks cover wide receivers; the strong safety covers the tight end; and the free safety provides roaming support.

Pass patterns: Any number of predetermined, much-practiced routes that the receivers run in collaboration with the pass-throwing quarterback. Pass patterns provide an element of predictability for both passer and receivers, and allow the receivers to run routes designed to confuse or outmaneuver the defenders without puzzling the passer.

Reverse: A deceptive play in which the quarterback takes the snap and gives it to a running back going in one direction, who then furtively hands the ball to a wide receiver headed in the opposite direction. Taking advantage of the onrushing defenders' momentary confusion, the wide receiver races behind the offensive line and then dashes downfield with the ball.

Tackle: When an opposing player forcibly grabs or blocks the player with the ball, forcing the ballcarrier to touch the ground with any part of his body except his hands. A successful tackle "downs" the ball and ends the play. In pro football, the ballcarrier is not down if he merely slips and falls; he may get up and continue running. In college, however, a slip-and-fall counts as a down.

Turnover: When possession of the football involuntarily changes from one team to the other because of a fumble or interception.

Zone defense: A defensive strategy in which the linebackers and defensive backs (cornerbacks and safeties) are each assigned an area of the field to cover and are responsible for pass coverage and/or tackling in those assigned "zones."

History

Tracing the lineage of football, its closest kin is rugby, started in England in 1823 by students at Rugby. They wanted to enliven the ball-kicking game of soccer by also carrying the ball.

Both soccer and rugby spread rapidly, crossing the Atlantic by the mid-1800s to American colleges. In 1876, a derivative rugby-type game called "football" was devised by a group of Harvard and Yale students. In the early 1880s, a series of new rules conceived by Walter Camp, a Yale student, was adopted. The resulting game resembled the modern sport of football, so Walter Camp is considered the sport's "father."

Football spread dramatically among American colleges during the 1890s, and by the end of World War I the pro game was established. Eleven teams formed the American Professional Football Association in 1920, which became the National Football League (NFL) in 1922. The NFL split into two divisions in 1933, the year of the first NFL championship game (Chicago Bears 23, New York Giants 21).

By 1950, several competitive leagues had come and gone, and it was not until 1960 that the American Football League challenged the NFL's supremacy. In 1966, the two leagues agreed to merge (consummated in 1970) under the NFL's name and to split into two conferences (American Football Conference and the National Football Conference). Each year since 1967, the conferences' best teams have collided in the Super Bowl, the most-watched event on television (nearly half of all U.S. households tune in).

Today, the NFL consists of 30 teams split into two conferences; each conference is divided into three divisions—the Eastern, Central, and Western. Each team plays 16 games during the regular 17-week season (early September through late December), then the teams with the best win-loss records challenge each other in the post-season playoffs. The top two teams duel in the Super Bowl (held in late January), which has been won three or more times by six teams—the Green Bay Packers, Dallas Cowboys, Washington Redskins, Pittsburgh Steelers, San Francisco 49ers, and Oakland Raiders (Raiders played as the Los Angeles Raiders when they won the Super Bowl in 1984). Befitting the era of big-bucks sports contracts, the average salary for an NFL player exceeds $700,000 a year; superstars make millions.

At the collegiate level, most football teams play within the National Collegiate Athletic Association (NCAA), divided into three divisions according to school size (the largest schools play in Division I) as well as subdivisions called regional conferences. During the regular season—September through November—each collegiate team plays 11 to 12 games. The team with the best record attains the title of conference champion. In late December and early January, the prestigious "bowl" games are held, and the best teams are invited to play. The best known of these special games include the Rose Bowl, Cotton Bowl, Orange Bowl, Fiesta Bowl, and Sugar Bowl.

NCAA divisions I-AA, II, and III determine a champion by playing a championship tournament. (The Division I-A champion is chosen by a poll of the sports media and of coaches.)

chapter four

ICE HOCKEY

Skating on ice and wielding long flat sticks, hockey players aggressively maneuver a puck across a sheet of ice to knock it into the opposing team's goal. Because goals are difficult to make and count only one point each, scores in this sport rarely go into the double digits.

Although professional hockey might at first seem difficult to follow because of its fast and unfamiliar action, the basic play is similar to two other popular sports, soccer and basketball. Two teams compete on a regulation playing area, with a goal at each end. The objective is to attack the opposing team's goal to score points.

The Rink

Played on a sheet of ice called the "rink," measuring 85 feet wide by 200 feet long (in the Olympics, 100 by 200 feet), the game's action is contained by "the boards," a retaining wall that surrounds the rink. A red line across the center of the rink divides it in two. Marked crosswise by two blue lines, the rink is also divided into thirds: two "end zones" and one "neutral zone." In each end zone, there is a goal cage (six feet wide and four feet tall) and a red goal line, which runs the width of the rink. There are also nine "face-off spots," four in each half of the rink and one in the middle.

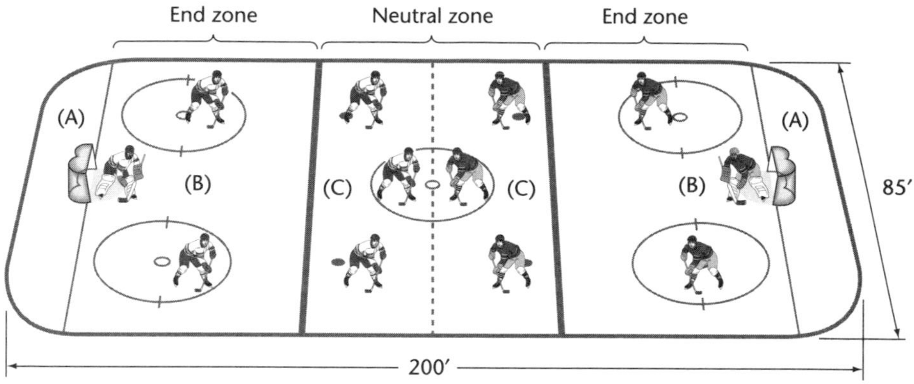

Figure 21. Each team consists of six players on the ice: (A) a goalie, (B) two defensemen, and (C) three forwards.

The Players

Each team can have six players on the ice at one time—three forwards, two defensemen, and one goalie (see Figure 21). While assigned positions are offensive or defensive, most of the players also assist in any capacity needed. In addition to the players on the ice, each team can have another 14 players in uniform on the bench to use as substitutes when on-ice players get tired, penalized, or hurt.

Goalie

Unlike his five teammates on the ice, the goalie (or goaltender) generally stays in one area of the rink. His sole job is to stop the puck from entering his team's goal cage, which he guards closely. He rarely skates away from the small marked-off area (called the "crease") in front of the cage. Because he must block the high-velocity puck, oftentimes with his body, he is the most heavily padded player on the team. As the only player allowed to catch and throw the puck, the goalie wears a big mitt on one hand and a padded blocking glove on the other. He also carries a broader stick than other players, and his arms and legs are heavily padded for blocking. He's the tough, sturdy, fearless type with an intimidating presence, a keen sense of anticipation, and very fast reflexes. A good goalie blocks up to 90 percent of opponents' shots on goal.

Defensemen

Commanding the end zone in front of the goalie are the two defensemen, one guarding the left side, the other the right. When the puck carrier from the opposing team enters into this zone (called the "attacking zone" of the puck-carrying team and the "defensive zone" of the defending team), it is the job of the defensemen to impede the carrier's progress and break up play by "checking" (blocking), by deflecting any pass or shot, and, if possible, by stealing the puck. Working together as a highly skilled team, they are the last line of defense before the goalie.

Defensemen are agile yet have plenty of strength for body blocking. They must be particularly good at skating backward because, as the puck carrier enters the attacking zone, a defenseman will typically position himself in front of the carrier and move with him, keeping his back to the goal. A good defenseman always tries to stay between the puck carrier and the goal, acting as a barrier and striving to thwart any attempt at scoring.

Forwards

Three players form the forward line—the center, the left wing, and the right wing. They are primarily responsible for an aggressive offense designed to carry the puck deep into their attacking zone (the opponent's defensive zone) and for attempting to shoot the puck for a goal.

> "You can't make it [in hockey] if you don't skate
> with your head, heart, and feet."
> *—Scotty Bowman, famed coach*

The center is usually the key player on the team and the most versatile. As the player who guides the offensive action, he is strong and imposing, yet quick on his skates and able to handle the puck with force and finesse. Although a good shot-maker, he will often pass the puck with split-second timing to one of the wings, who then attempts to score the goal.

The wings, both left and right, are usually the fastest skaters and the best shooters. Working in concert with the center, they are quick thinkers who keep relentless pressure on the opposing goalie and defensemen.

The Action

A game is divided into three 20-minute "periods," which are separated by two 15-minute intermissions. In case of a tie, the teams play a five-minute "sudden death" overtime period; the first team to score wins.

Play begins at center ice with a "face-off." On opposite sides of the "spot," the center from each team waits for the referee to drop the puck onto the ice. Once it drops, each player immediately tries to knock it with his stick to a teammate. This procedure is repeated after each goal is scored and after certain penalties.

The team that gains possession of the puck after the face-off immediately tries to maneuver it toward the opposing team's goal. This is done by passing it from one teammate to another or by one player "stickhandling it up ice" (pushing it along the ice with his stick). Meanwhile, the defending team's players try to intercept passes or steal the puck.

As the attacking team advances the puck into the end zone, play quickens and intensifies. Upon seeing an opening, the player with the puck instantly attempts to smack the puck through for a goal. At the same time, the defending players are doing everything in their power to block the shot.

Shooting and Passing the Puck

Shots at the goal cage are usually made with one of two swings—the wrist shot or the slap shot.

With the wily wrist shot, the player takes a short backswing and then, without lifting the blade of the stick off the ice, snaps it forward against the puck. Because the wrist shot can be executed quickly, it is difficult for the opposing team to anticipate. A more controlled and accurate shot, it is used much more often than the slap.

The real crowd pleaser, however, is the slap shot. Hit almost like a golf swing, with a full windup and follow-through, it is the big power shot. What it loses in accuracy it gains in speed and intimidation. A well-hit puck can travel 85 to 100 mph and is very difficult to see, much less block.

The quickest goal from the start of a pro hockey game was made in five seconds. It happened between the Winnipeg Jets and the St. Louis Blues on December 20, 1981.

Both shots can be made so that the puck either glides along the ice (hit "flat") or flies in the air (a "flip"). The shot or pass struck flat is executed with the blade tilted down, and the puck is hit near the heel of the blade. With the flip, the blade is tilted up and makes contact with the puck near the blade's toe. A little more wrist action is used with the flip to make the puck rise higher, but given too much flip, the puck can soar over the boards and into the crowd.

Passing the puck from one teammate to another is a very important aspect of hockey because it is the quickest way to maneuver the puck and outwit the opposition. The three basic passes are the "flat pass" (the puck glides along the ice), the "flip pass" (the puck rises off the ice), and the "drop pass." In the drop pass, the player skating with the puck suddenly leaves it behind for another teammate to take immediate control of.

Checking

The "body check" is the main reason for hockey's rough reputation. It is a forceful block designed to knock the stuffing out of the player with the puck and give control of it to the opposing player. A check is perfectly legal, so long as it is only delivered against the player with the puck (see Figure 22).

A defensive player can legally deliver a body check only with the shoulder, hip, or torso. An effective body check will knock the puck carrier down or away from the puck, spoil the offensive play, and give the defense a good chance to steal the puck.

Figure 22. A player can legally deliver a forceful block, or body check, to an opposing player only when that player has the puck.

The "stick check" is another defensive move designed to steal the puck or at least knock it away from the offensive carrier. To execute a stick check, the defensive player tries to knock the puck away from the carrier with a "poke" (a one-handed stab at the puck with his stick) or a "sweep" (sweeping his stick blade along the ice at the puck in front of the carrier).

Penalties

To prevent hockey from becoming a donnybrook on ice, there are many rules fortified with stiff penalties. Most are meant to discourage unnecessary roughness and injury; all are enforced by three on-ice officials—the referee and two linesmen. Just outside the rink are several other officials including the game timekeeper, the penalty timekeeper, the official scorer, two goal judges, and two penalty bench attendants.

Basically, the rules state that a player is not allowed to hit another with his stick or even to raise his stick in a menacing, intimidating manner. The various illegal stickhandlings are aptly named: "butt ending," "cross-checking," "high sticking," "spearing," and "slashing."

Players can also be penalized for body checking an offensive player who is not carrying the puck (called "interference") or for intentionally crashing into a defensive player ("charging" and "unnecessary roughness").

When asked if he had ever broken his nose, hockey great Gordie Howe replied, "No, but eleven other guys did."

All these illegal acts momentarily stop the play and are punishable with a variety of penalties. Most include the temporary banishment of the offending player to the penalty bench or "box," which is a glassed-in booth beside the rink. While he is in the box, the penalized team must continue the game with only five players. This is called playing "shorthanded." During this time, the opposing team outnumbers the penalized team and tries its best to score while having the temporary advantage. This is called "power play" hockey and results in a goal being scored about 15 to 20 percent of the time. The rules permit no more than two players from a team to be in the penalty box at one time; if a third player is sent to the penalty box, his team can put in a substitute to maintain at least four players on the ice.

After play has been stopped because of a penalty, it resumes with a face-off, usually at the face-off spot closest to where the violation occurred. The basic penalty categories are:

- *Minor:* A violation such as holding or tripping an opponent, or "hooking" him (holding him back with the blade of the stick). A player with a minor penalty must spend two minutes in the box, and his team must play shorthanded for the duration of the penalty or until a goal is scored against them.

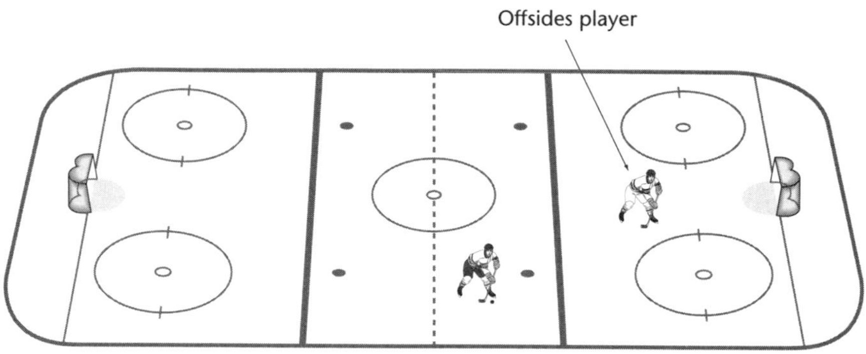

Figure 23. The puck must always be carried or shot into the attacking zone before other offensive teammates may enter it. "Offsides" is called when an offensive player crosses the blue line into the attacking zone (the opposition's end zone) ahead of the puck. The penalty is a face-off.

- *Major:* A more serious violation, usually involving fighting and/or illegal use of the stick. The penalty is five minutes in the box, and the team must play shorthanded for the entire five minutes. Depending on the severity of the violation, a major foul can eliminate the offending player from the game.

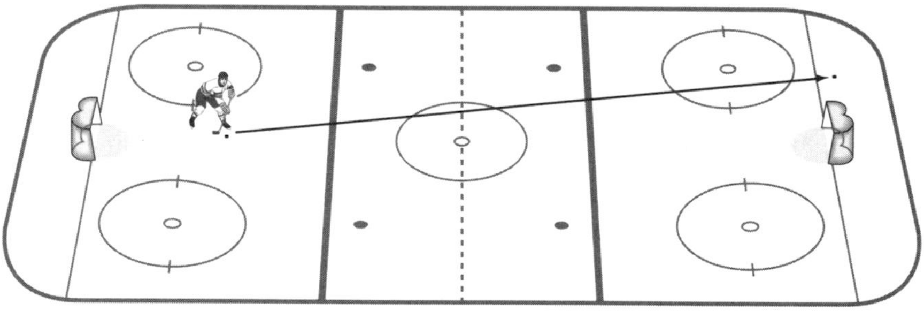

Figure 24. If players were allowed to slam the puck from one end of the rink to the other, not much hockey would get played, and the sport would deteriorate into boring monotony. Therefore, if a player hits the puck from his half of the rink across the goal line of the opposing team, an "icing the puck" violation is called if a player on the opposing team touches it before a player from the team that shot it. If icing is called, play is stopped and the puck is faced off in the offending team's end zone. (While a team is playing shorthanded, however, it may ice the puck without penalty.)

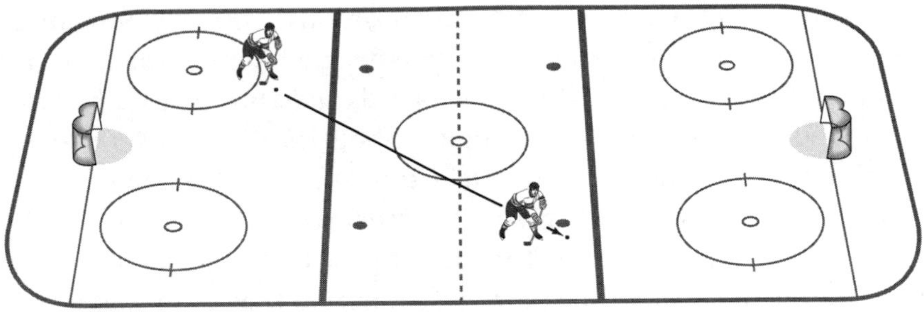

Figure 25. An "offside pass" is called against a player who passes the puck from within his team's end zone to a teammate on the other side of the red center line. The penalty is a face-off in the offending team's end zone.

- *Misconduct:* Usually given for cursing or threatening one of the officials. The penalty is 10 minutes in the box, but the team can use a substitute player during that time.
- *Match:* Levied for deliberately trying to hurt another player. The guilty player is ejected from the game, and his team must play shorthanded for five minutes before putting in a substitute.
- *Penalty shot:* Awarded if the puck carrier in the "attacking zone" has an unobstructed shot at the goal, but is fouled from behind as he attempts to make the shot. The fouled player is given the puck at center ice, and all other players leave the ice except for the opposing goalie. The puck carrier goes against the goalie, one-on-one, and is allowed a one-shot attempt on the goal. A penalty shot always provides high drama, but more than half the time the goalie blocks the shot.

Three other violations that happen frequently during a game are "offsides," "icing the puck," and "offside pass," as shown in the illustrations (Figures 23, 24, and 25).

Numbers Guide

In addition to the score, the electronic scoreboard at a hockey game shows which of the three periods is being played and the time remaining in that 20-minute period.

During penalty periods, the scoreboard also displays how much penalty time remains—and therefore how much longer the intensity of a power play will last. Most scoreboards also show the cumulative number of "shots on goal" (attempted shots to score) by each team.

The sports sections of most metro newspapers list the scores of pro hockey games, usually giving the final score and sometimes the goals by period as well as the total number of shots on goal by period. Some report the exact time during each period that goals and penalties occurred. These statistics provide insights into the ebb and flow of the game and, comparing the number of shots on goal, which team dominated.

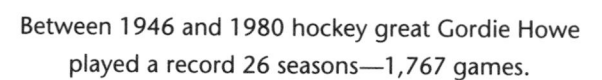

Between 1946 and 1980 hockey great Gordie Howe played a record 26 seasons—1,767 games.

Strategy

Once a team gains possession of the puck, it will advance toward the opposing team's goal with the three forwards in front and the two defensemen trailing about a zone behind; that team's goalie, of course, stays behind to guard the goal. Often, the center will skate with the puck into the attacking zone while the two wings swiftly fan out to each side in anticipation of a pass. Maneuvering the puck back and forth, the offensive forwards will try to deceive the defenders and draw them away from the goal to take a clear shot.

The best area from which to shoot is directly in front of the cage—an area called the "slot"—because the defending goalie is forced to protect the entire mouth of the cage. For this reason, defense gets roughest when the attacking puck carrier enters the slot.

During a power play (when one team is shorthanded because it has a player in the penalty box), the game intensifies dramatically. The team with the advantage will apply tremendous pressure to the opposing team and will attempt as many shots as possible during the penalty time. Usually, it will try to pass the puck to its unguarded player for a clean shot at the goal.

Meanwhile, the team with the disadvantage will resort to defensive "penalty-killing" hockey. Trying to compensate for its handicap, the team will play extra hard and ice the puck—the only time icing is legal—as frequently as possible to keep it out of its defending zone. The shorthanded team will often form a four-man "box" defense in front of its goalie to give maximum coverage to the slot area. Sometimes the team waging a power play will attack with four forwards and retain only one defenseman with the goalie.

Equipment

Hockey is a game of sudden and unexpected moves that can lead to bone-jarring impact. Accidents happen, and injuries can be serious. Therefore, all players wear protective helmets, gloves, and plenty of body padding underneath their uniforms. There is padding to protect their shoulders, ribs and sternum, shins and elbows, and more to protect their hips, groin, and lower back (see Figure 26). The

Figure 26. With players averaging 200 pounds, hockey can be a rough game and injuries are not uncommon. Players wear thick gloves, safety helmets, and lots of protective body padding.

Definition of a puck: "A hard rubber disk that hockey players strike when they can't hit one another."
—*Jimmy Cannon, sportswriter*

goaltender's padding is heavier than that of the other players and includes especially thick leg pads; he also wears a face guard that is attached to his helmet.

The hockey skate is a stiff boot with a blade on the bottom that is slightly curved, or "rockered," to permit quick turns and stops. The gleaming steel blade is kept sharp to bite into the ice for the best possible traction. On the boot at the back of the ankle is a special protective strip of leather to guard the Achilles tendon from being sliced by an errant stick or skate blade (see Figure 27).

Hockey sticks are usually made of hardwood, but they can also be fiberglass, aluminum, or graphite. The shaft can be no longer than 63 inches and the blade no longer than $12^1/_2$ inches (the goalie's stick is a little broader with a slightly longer blade). The blade is often wrapped in tape to help guide the puck.

The puck, sometimes called the "biscuit," is a black disk of solid vulcanized rubber. It measures three inches across, is one inch thick, and weighs about six ounces. The puck is frozen before a game to keep it from bouncing too much along the ice during play.

Figure 27. The hockey boot provides support and protection while the slightly curved blade facilitates quick, sharp turns on the ice.

Ice: The Cold, Hard Facts

In hockey, there is good ice and bad ice; some rinks just skate and play better than others. This is usually due to the nature of the ice itself. An ideal hockey surface provides a hard, smooth sheet of ice. Hard ice, with an optimum temperature of about 19° F (–7.2° C), permits a player to get a good bite with his skate blades for quick turns, stops, and starts. Smooth ice, which is maintained by the careful grooming of an expert, allows the puck to glide fast and accurately and gives the players a predictable surface on which to skate.

The foundation of most hockey rinks is a giant slab of concrete, beneath which lies a network of refrigeration pipes to freeze the concrete and the water poured over it. To form a playing surface, a thin coating of water is sprayed over the concrete and then frozen. After that surface has been painted white, a quarter-inch of water is sprayed over it and frozen. Then the lines are put down using paint, strips of special paper, or cloth. After a final half-inch of water is applied and frozen, the surface is ready for play. Depending upon the facility, the entire process takes about a day and costs approximately $8,000, including the cost of water (about 15,000 gallons), paint, labor, and electricity.

Most rink surfaces are groomed by an odd-looking machine with an odder name—the Zamboni. It is named for Frank Zamboni, a Californian who combined an Army jeep, a water tank, and a cutting blade to invent the first ice-resurfacing machine in 1949. The newfangled machine was popularized by the great Olympic figure-skating champion Sonja Henie, who took it on her ice show tours all over the world to ensure a smooth, gleaming surface wherever she performed.

The Zamboni prepares a perfect playing surface before the hockey game and again during the two 15-minute intermissions. It automatically shaves the ice, gathers the shavings, and then lays down a thin layer of hot water, which quickly freezes to form a smooth, glassy surface. The operator drives the four-wheeled Zamboni around the rink in ever-tightening circles while making fine adjustments to the shaving blades and water nozzles. Performing a job that once took one and a half hours, this ingenious machine can resurface a rink in less than 10 minutes.

History

The origin of ice hockey is hazy, but most sports historians trace it back to eastern Canada during the 1860s, when British soldiers came up with a game of batting a ball on ice between two goal lines. A decade later students at Montreal's McGill University set down some basic rules. In 1893 hockey was introduced in the United States at the collegiate level with a match between Yale and Johns Hopkins. That same year the Canadian governor general, Lord Stanley of Preston, first offered a silver bowl to the best hockey team in Canada. A century later the Stanley Cup remains the preeminent prize among all the professional teams of the National Hockey League.

Over the past 25 years, the coveted Stanley Cup has been won at least four times by the Montreal Canadiens, New York Islanders, and Edmonton Oilers.

By the turn of the century, the sport was firmly established in Canada and was beginning to gain popularity in the United States, particularly in New York. In 1909, the National Hockey Association formed with teams from Toronto, Ottawa, and Montreal. It disbanded in 1917, and the National Hockey League (NHL) was formed and gradually grew to oversee and govern the professional sport in North America. By 1981, the NHL was composed of 21 teams (27 teams at this printing), and the league's plans call for 30 by the year 2000.

The sport's heritage also includes a proud tradition in the Olympics. It was first included as a medal sport in the 1920 Olympic Games, and has been part of the Winter Olympics since its inauguration in 1924. Beginning with the 1998 Winter Olympics, women's hockey teams have also competed.

chapter five

SOCCER

Because it's easy to understand and loaded with nonstop excitement, soccer is the world's most popular sport. It isn't a major spectator sport in the United States yet, but many experts predict that this will change dramatically in the foreseeable future.

Everywhere except the United States, soccer is called "football." There is scant similarity between U.S. football and soccer, however, even though the two sports share some common terminology such as "tackle," "kickoff," and "fullback." Each sport defines these and other terms very differently.

The Basics

Two teams—each with 11 seemingly tireless players—compete on a large, grassy field with a goal at each end (see Figure 28). In professional soccer, a regulation field measures 120 yards long by 75 yards wide. Each team defends one of the goals, and the object of the game is to advance the soccer ball into the opponent's goal to score a point.

Players can use any part of their bodies to hit or kick the ball except for their hands or arms. Therefore, players are remarkably skilled at maneuvering the ball with their feet. The rules prohibit tripping, kicking, pushing, or holding another player.

For each team, one player (called the "goalkeeper," "keeper," or "goaltender") stays in a marked-off area (called the "penalty area") in

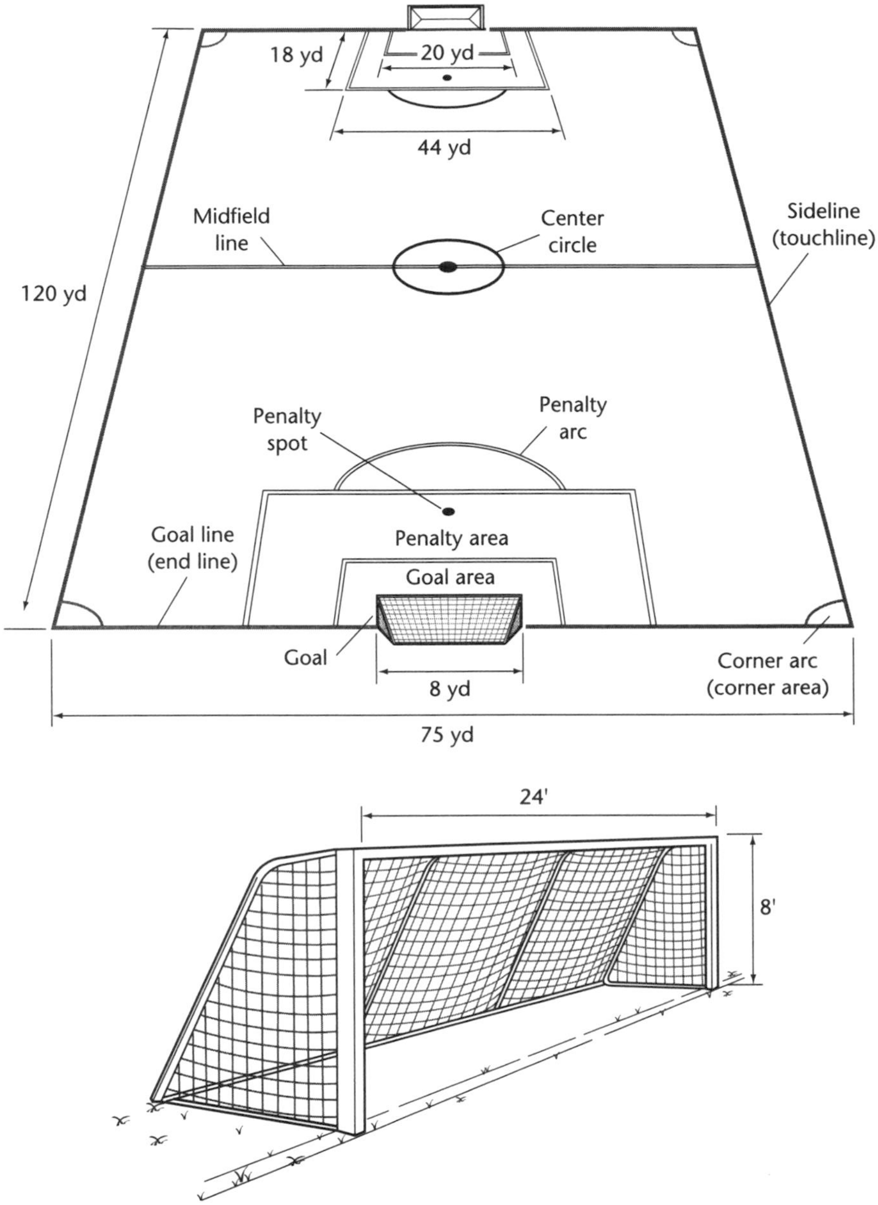

Figure 28. A soccer field for professional play measures 120 yards long by 75 yards wide (70 percent bigger than a U.S. football field). The mouth of the netted goal cage at each end is 8 feet tall and 24 feet wide.

front of the goal; he is the team's last line of defense against an attempted score by the opposition. The other players run up and down the field (as much as 10 miles during a match), employing offensive or defensive tactics depending on which team has possession of the ball.

The goalkeeper is the one player on each team permitted to catch or block the ball with his hands and arms, so long as he is within the rectangular 18-by-44-yard "penalty area" in front of the goal. An opposing player may not attempt to take away the ball as long as the keeper is holding it with his hands.

The World Cup has been held in the United States only once, in 1994.

A match consists of two 45-minute halves (divided by a 15-minute intermission) and no formal time-outs. It begins with a coin toss to determine which team gets the ball first and which goal each team will defend. For the "kickoff," both teams gather on opposite sides of the midfield circle and face the opponent's goal. The referee places the ball in the middle of the circle, and a member of the team with first possession kicks it to a fellow teammate. (After each score, a kickoff is held with initial possession given to the team just scored against.)

Immediately following the kickoff, the team in possession of the ball continuously attempts to maneuver the ball toward the opponent's goal to score (or to "make a goal"). Meanwhile, the other team tries to defend its goal against the attackers by blocking shots and by attempting to gain possession of the ball either by intercepting a pass or by stealing the ball—called "tackling" when a defensive player uses his foot to maneuver the ball away from an opponent (see Figure 29). After the first half, the teams switch goals.

Figure 29. A defender may attempt to separate an offensive player from the ball by kicking it away with his foot. This is called "tackling." When tackling, physical contact is legal so long as it is incidental to the defensive player's attempt to kick the ball.

Advancing the Ball

A player can advance the ball by (1) dribbling it (a rapid succession of short, controlled kicks while running) or by (2) passing it to a teammate (either by kicking the ball or by "heading" it—striking the ball in midair with his head, usually his forehead). Pros and top-ranked amateurs are incredibly skillful at dribbling and can pass and shoot with amazing accuracy.

"The rules [of soccer] are very simple. Basically, it's this: If it moves, kick it; if it doesn't move, kick it until it does."

—*Phil Woosnam, Commissioner, North American Soccer League*

Dribbling is accomplished by lightly tapping or nudging the ball with the toe or sides of the shoe (see Figure 30). To kick a long pass, the ball is booted off the hard, bony instep of the foot. For short passes, the player usually kicks the ball with the side of his or her foot.

Since a player isn't allowed to intentionally touch the ball with his arms or hands, he receives a pass by gently blocking the ball down to the ground with his chest, thigh, or foot (called "controlling" or "trapping" the ball). He can then proceed to dribble, pass, or shoot it.

Figure 30. "Dribbling" is one way a player can move the ball. He controls the ball as he runs using a series of short, gentle kicks with the toe or sides of his feet. Pros are remarkably skilled at dribbling and can often maneuver the ball past several defenders in this manner.

Scoring

One point is scored when the ball passes through the mouth of the opponent's goal, which is positioned at the center of the goal line. The goal mouth is 24 feet wide and 8 feet tall. A cage—made of nylon netting and attached to the back of the goal—is designed to capture the ball when it gets hit through this wide opening.

When an opposing player approaches the goal with the ball in an attempt to score, the goalkeeper positions himself in front of the goal to obstruct shots. In order to more effectively block the attempted shot, the goalkeeper usually advances toward the opposing player to cut off the best angles for scoring (see Figure 31). Because scoring a goal is so difficult, it's unusual for more than three or four points to be scored in an entire match.

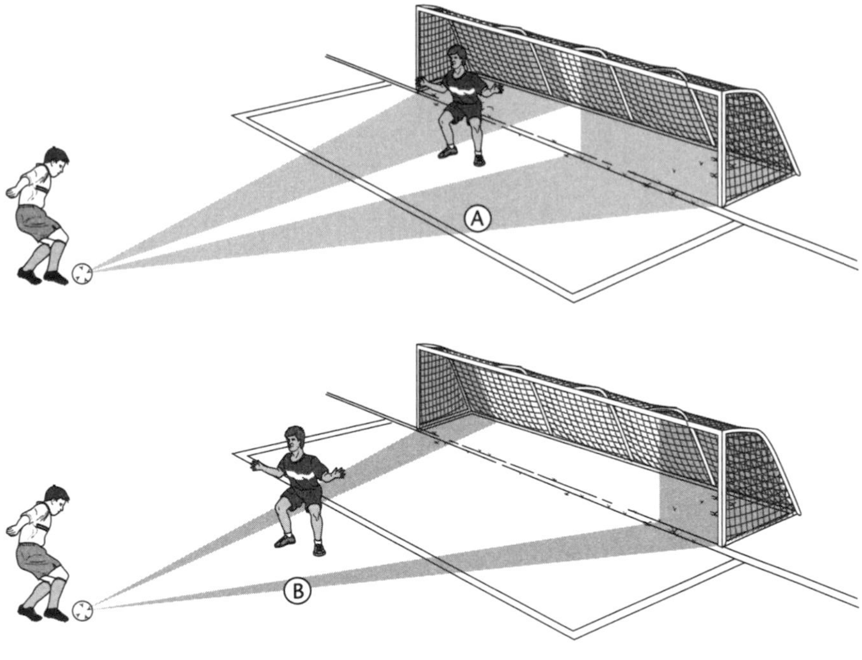

Figure 31. When a goalkeeper moves away from the goal (from A to B) to confront an approaching opponent with the ball, the goalkeeper obscures a larger area of the goal mouth, thereby cutting down the opponent's chance to kick a goal.

If the score is tied at the end of a match, then the contest is either declared a draw or play continues until a winner emerges. In many pro leagues, in all championship matches, and in tournaments where winners must be decided, a tie is broken in one of two ways:

1. Play goes into two 15-minute overtime periods. Whichever team scores first wins the match. This is called a "golden goal" overtime (or "sudden death" in other sports). If still tied at the end of overtime, the game is decided by a tiebreaker (called a "shootout"), which is an exciting series of five penalty kicks by each team.
2. The game goes directly to a shootout (penalty kicks).

The Players

Except for the goalkeeper, who stays on guard in front of his team's goal, the players are responsible for both offensive and defensive maneuvers across the entire field and for providing backup support for one another. In pro soccer, a coach may substitute one player for another only three times during an entire game, so substitutions are used sparingly, usually for a player who gets seriously injured or is playing very poorly. (In collegiate soccer, a coach can make unlimited substitutions during a game. This is the most significant rule difference between collegiate and pro soccer.)

Although all pros are skillful players and very versatile, each has a basic job to perform. But because professional play is very fluid and spontaneous, players' responsibilities often overlap (this overlapping system of play is sometimes called "total soccer"). As a basic structure, players are positioned in three rows, as follows (see Figure 32).

Forwards

Usually two or three players, forwards are positioned farthest from their own goal and are responsible for attacking the opponent's goal and scoring points. With three forwards, the one in the middle is the "striker"; he's usually the strongest and takes most of the shots. The

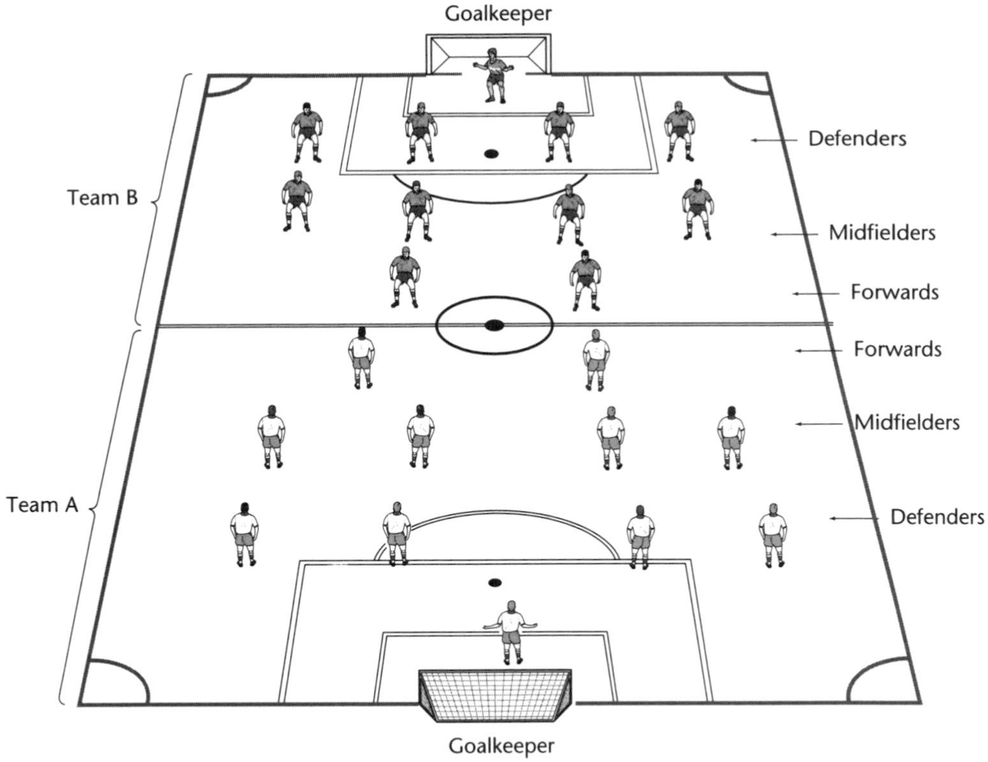

Figure 32. These are the basic player positions for each team. The defenders are responsible for breaking up the opponent's offensive plays near the goal; the midfielders assist both the defenders and forwards; and the forwards are responsible for attacking the opposition's goal and for scoring. The goalkeeper blocks the opposition's shots to score.

other two are the "wings" or "wingers," who are fast runners and excellent dribblers and passers. Wingers maneuver the ball deep into the opponent's territory and either pass the ball to the striker for scoring opportunities or attempt goal shots themselves.

Midfielders (or Halfbacks)

Usually four players, they are strategically positioned between the forwards and defenders. Midfielders are mainly playmakers between the offensive and defensive players and, descriptive of their function, are sometimes called "linkmen." They often assist the forwards for offensive attacks and assist the defenders for defensive actions.

Defenders

Usually three to five defenders play between the midfielders and the goalkeeper. "Fullbacks" play to the outside left and right and cover attacking wingers. "Central defenders" cover the left and right middle of the field in front of the goalkeeper. In some defensive formations, these two central players line up one in front of the other. The player in front is called the "stopper," and usually covers the opposition's striker; the other, called the "sweeper," roves behind his fellow defenders in a support role and to offer resistance before the opposition reaches the keeper.

Goalkeeper (Also Keeper, Goaltender, or Goalie)

Positioned behind these three rows of teammates is the goalkeeper, perhaps the most critical player to a team's success. His main job is to block opponents' shots for goals. Because it's impossible for him to cover the entire 24-foot-wide mouth of the goal, he must have a keen sense of anticipation and accurately read offensive plays as they develop in order to position himself for an effective defense. Bold and tough, he is the only player allowed to use his arms and hands to catch, throw, or deflect the ball.

In addition to defending his team's goal, the goalkeeper performs another important function. He relays (or "distributes") the balls he catches to his teammates by throwing, kicking, or rolling the ball to them.

Fouls and Infractions

Soccer rules are designed primarily to protect players from injury and to keep the game moving. The rules punish poor sportsmanship, dangerous play, and intentional delays.

Out-of-Bounds

When the ball goes out-of-bounds—either across the sideline (often called "touchline") or across the goal line (often called "end line")—play is briefly stopped and possession of the ball is automatically given to the team which did not touch it last. Here's how and where:

1. If the ball goes out-of-bounds across the touchline, the team which did not touch it last is given a "throw-in" from the point where it went out-of-bounds. For a throw-in, the player stands just outside the touchline and, using both hands, makes an overhead pass to a teammate inbounds.
2. If it goes out-of-bounds across the end line (but not into the goal), it's put back into play in one of two ways, depending on which team knocked it out-of-bounds.
   - If the defense knocked it out-of-bounds, then the offense is given a "corner kick" from the nearest corner of the field (no opponents are allowed within 10 yards). Corner kicks are usually used as scoring opportunities. The kicker either attempts a "banana ball," which curves toward the goal, or more often kicks to a teammate in front of the goal who then attempts to head or kick the ball in to score.
   - If the offense knocked it out-of-bounds, then the defense is given a "goal kick"—that is, a defensive player is permitted to kick the ball downfield and away from his goal area (no opponents are allowed within the penalty area until he's kicked the ball).

Note that if the player in possession of the ball steps out-of-bounds but the ball remains inbounds, then play continues normally. A player's position in relation to the boundary lines is irrelevant.

Fouls

Fouls are called in response to dangerous or obstructive play and to unsportsmanlike or abusive behavior. Shouldering and incidental contact are permitted if the defensive player is clearly making a play for the ball, but not to block or injure the opponent. When a foul is called, the referee awards the offended team one of three types of free kicks:

1. *Indirect free kick:* These kicks are awarded for the least serious infractions, such as charging or intentionally obstructing an opponent. From the point where the infraction occurred, a player from the offended team is given a free kick. If used to attempt a goal, the shot must be made indirectly (i.e., the free kick must be booted to a teammate, who can then attempt a shot to score). The goalkeeper is permitted to attempt to block the shot.

2. *Direct free kick:* These kicks are awarded for more serious infractions such as kicking, striking, holding, or pushing an opponent or for touching the ball with the hands or arms. From the point where the infraction occurred, a player from the offended team is given a free kick. If used to attempt a goal, the shot can be made directly, but the defensive team is allowed to form a "wall" between the kicker and the goal. A wall usually consists of two to six players standing shoulder to shoulder in front of the kicker but at least 10 yards from him. By partially blocking a clear shot at the goal, a wall assists the goalkeeper's defense.

3. *Penalty kick:* If any of these more serious fouls are committed by the defensive team within the penalty area, then a player from the offended team is awarded a penalty kick, which is booted from the marked spot that is 12 yards away from the mouth of the goal and directly in front of it. In this dramatic one-on-one situation, only the keeper is permitted to defend the goal against the penalty kick; all other players must stand at least 10 yards away. (Almost all penalty kicks score goals.)

In addition to awarding free kicks for fouls or violations, the on-field officials are empowered to levy (or "book") a yellow or red card against a player for serious misconduct and/or unsportsmanlike behavior (the official holds up a yellow or red card to signal this disciplinary action). A yellow card is a stern caution. A red card immediately ejects the offending player, and his team must play the rest of the game one player short, or "shorthanded." (If a player is booked for two yellow cards, he is ejected and, as for a red-card violation, cannot be replaced.)

Time Clock

Oddly enough, the scoreboard clock for international soccer games shows only the unofficial time remaining in each 45-minute half. (The referee holds the official game clock.) In U.S. pro soccer, the scoreboard and referee clocks are the same.

In international play, the clock doesn't stop when play does for out-of-bounds balls, after scores, or to settle fouls. At the discretion of the referee, however, time can be accounted for when play stops for an injured player or if the referee believes a team has intentionally delayed the game, and he adds this time to the end of the game once the unofficial clock runs out. In the United States, the referee sometimes stops the clock for injuries.

Strategy

As a general rule, the offensive team tries to funnel its attack toward the front of the opponent's goal for the best scoring opportunities. A frontal attack provides the shooter with the broadest exposure to the goal mouth (see Figure 33). Defenders, of course, work hardest to obstruct a frontal attack and attempt to force play to the outside, where the shooting angles toward the goal are much more limited.

Some teams are particularly good at offensive play, others at defense. Championship teams are usually strong at both, but may have a bias for one or the other depending on the players' expertise.

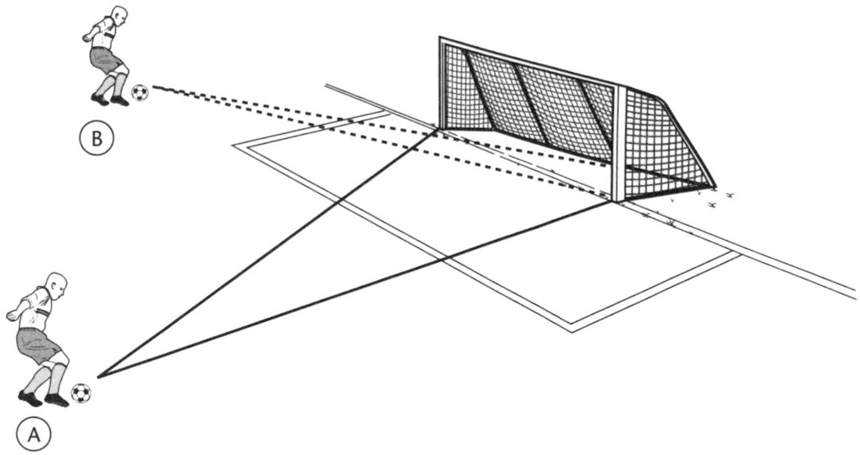

Figure 33. The best place to attempt to score is (A) directly in front of the goal. The shooter's angle of opportunity is much smaller when (B) attacking from the side. Therefore, a frontal attack usually meets much more resistance from the defensive team.

To leverage his or her team's strength for tactical advantage, the coach aligns the players on the field in a specific formation—notably the 4-3-3, variations of 4-4-2, 3-5-2, and 5-4-1—also called a "system" of play. For example, a forceful, aggressive team might use three defenders, five midfielders, and two forwards (called a 3-5-2 formation). In this formation, two to four midfielders might move up temporarily to join the forwards to intensify an attack. A defense-oriented team might adopt a 5-4-1 formation (five defenders including a sweeper, four midfielders, and just one forward, or striker) to provide plenty of fortification in front of its goalkeeper and goal. One of the more popular formations is the 4-4-2 (shown in Figure 32). This balanced alignment provides a team with effective firepower on offense (when at least two midfielders often join the forwards to attack) and sufficient fortification on defense (when midfielders drop back to help support the defenders and goalie).

The Guinness sports record for juggling a soccer ball is 19 hours, 5 minutes, and 31 seconds, set by Ricardinho Neves in 1994. The record for heading a soccer ball is 8 hours, 12 minutes, and 25 seconds, set by Godzerzi Maakharadze in 1996.

In addition to following a particular system of play, each team usually displays a particular "style" of play. A direct style, for example, emphasizes aggressiveness and is characterized by a lot of long passes ("air balls") and attacks on goal. An indirect style relies on finesse, artful dribbling, short pass combinations, tricky ballhandling, and other deceptive maneuvers.

Equipment

A soccer ball is pressure-inflated and covered in a patchwork of starkly-designed leather (or synthetic) panels, which help players gauge the ball's spin and velocity. About nine inches in diameter, the ball is slightly smaller than a basketball.

Pro soccer players—who average about 5' 10", 165 pounds—wear surprisingly little padding for protection against injury. All players wear shin guards as well as short-sleeved shirts, shorts, knee socks, and soft-leather shoes with rubber cleats. The goalkeepers also wear gloves to grip the ball and protect their hands. The goalkeeper's shirt is a different color from his teammates' so that he can be easily identified.

Other Important Stuff

Bicycle kick: Spectacular move in which a player leaps into the air to kick the ball over his head and backward. Also called a scissors kick.

Charge: While making a play for the ball, to shoulder the player in possession of the ball in order to knock him off balance. (Illegal if used from behind or against a player without the ball.)

Clear: As a defensive move, to kick or head the ball well away from the goal area.

Corner arc (or corner area): The quarter-circle area (one-yard radius) in each corner of the field from which corner kicks are made.

Cross: To pass the ball from one side of the field to the other.

Hat trick: A rare achievement, when a player scores three or more goals in a single game.

Man-to-man: A defensive tactic whereby each defender is assigned to cover (or "mark") a specific forward from the opposing team.

Offside: A violation that is called if the offensive player with the ball passes it to a teammate when there are fewer than two opposing players (including the goalkeeper) between that teammate and the goal. Play is stopped and the team against which the foul was committed is awarded an indirect free kick from where the infringement took place. Offside is not called if the pass is made directly from a corner kick, a throw-in, a goal kick, or from the offensive team's half of the field.

Pelé: Edson Arantes do Nascimento, a superstar of the '50s, '60s, and '70s. This famous Brazilian is considered the greatest soccer player ever.

Through pass: A pass to a teammate in open space and behind a defender.

Wall pass: A common offensive play whereby Player A (with the ball) kicks the ball to a nearby teammate; Player A then dodges around his opponent and, once in the clear, regains the ball almost immediately through a short, quick pass from the teammate (just like a give-and-go in basketball).

Zone: A defensive tactic whereby each defender is assigned to cover a specific area (zone) of the field and to be responsible for guarding any offensive player who enters that zone.

History

Had it not been for the independent-mindedness of nineteenth-century Americans—who were more inclined to invent new sports than to adopt British games—soccer and cricket may well have become predominant spectator sports in the United States instead of homegrown pastimes such as football, baseball, and basketball.

Team sports similar to soccer date back to ancient Egypt, China, Greece, and Rome. An early English version was unsuccessfully banned by King Edward III in 1365 for absorbing too much of the populace's time and energies.

By the early 1800s, the game had evolved to bear resemblance to the modern game, and the first complete set of rules was written at Cambridge University in 1846. (In 1823, an offshoot of the game, called rugby, was developed by English students. In the late 1870s and early 1880s, American collegiate students devised the game of American football from rugby.) The first soccer association was formed in England in 1863 to standardize the rules of the sport, and teams were formally restricted to 11 players in 1870.

Because of Britain's worldwide commercial and military influence in the nineteenth century, the sport spread rapidly and by World War I was established throughout Europe, South America, and in parts of Asia. In 1904, the Federation Internationale de Football Association (FIFA) was established by a group of European countries to oversee and govern the sport.

In 1994 Brazil won an unprecedented fourth World Cup title (the others were captured in 1958, 1962, and 1970).

FIFA organized and still coordinates the prestigious World Cup, which is held every four years. It is the most-watched sporting event on the planet. First played in 1930, the World Cup has recently been held in France (1998), the United States (1994), Italy (1990), Mexico (1986), Spain (1982), and Argentina (1978). In 2002, it will be held in both Japan and South Korea.

Historically, the strongest World Cup teams have hailed from Brazil, Germany, Italy, and Argentina. Each of nearly 200 countries carefully assembles a "national team"—composed mostly of professional players given leave by their teams—to participate in World Cup competitions. The U.S. Soccer Federation organizes America's national teams for men and women.

The Women's World Cup, started in 1991 by FIFA, is also held every four years, scheduled the year after the men's. The first was held in China, the second in Sweden (1995). The United States was chosen to host the event in 1999.

Professional soccer, although long viable in many other countries, has had a rocky history in the United States. Pro teams were unsuccessfully launched in the United States in the 1920s, 1930s, 1960s, 1970s, and 1980s. In 1996, Major League Soccer (MLS) was organized and has grown to include 12 pro teams. As soccer's popularity continues to grow in the United States, MLS's television contracts and corporate sponsorships gain strength as well.

Soccer is now America's most popular youth-participation sport, and many observers predict that its appeal as a spectator sport will mushroom as these youthful players reach adulthood.

Part II

INDIVIDUAL SPORTS

chapter six

BOWLING

The object of bowling—to skillfully roll a ball to knock down a formation of pins—has challenged man since ancient times. It requires smooth, fluid control and targeted concentration.

The modern sport of "tenpins" is the most popular form of bowling in America. It's played across the country in approximately 7,000 certified bowling centers with 138,000 lanes. At the professional level of play, the sport attracts millions of television viewers nationwide.

How It's Played

Tenpins is played on a long, narrow lane ("alley") of polished wood (see Figure 34). At one end of the lane is a 15-foot extension called the "approach," where the player takes four or five steps in preparation for bowling the ball. At the foul line, he or she releases the ball down the lane toward a triangular formation of upright pins 60 feet away. The player receives cumulative points for the number of pins knocked down throughout the game.

A game is divided into 10 segments called "frames," and each player is given up to two attempts per frame to knock down a set of 10 pins. All pins are reset after each player has completed a frame. After all players have completed 10 frames, the player with the most points wins that game. In a four-day championship tournament, the winner will bowl up to 56 games.

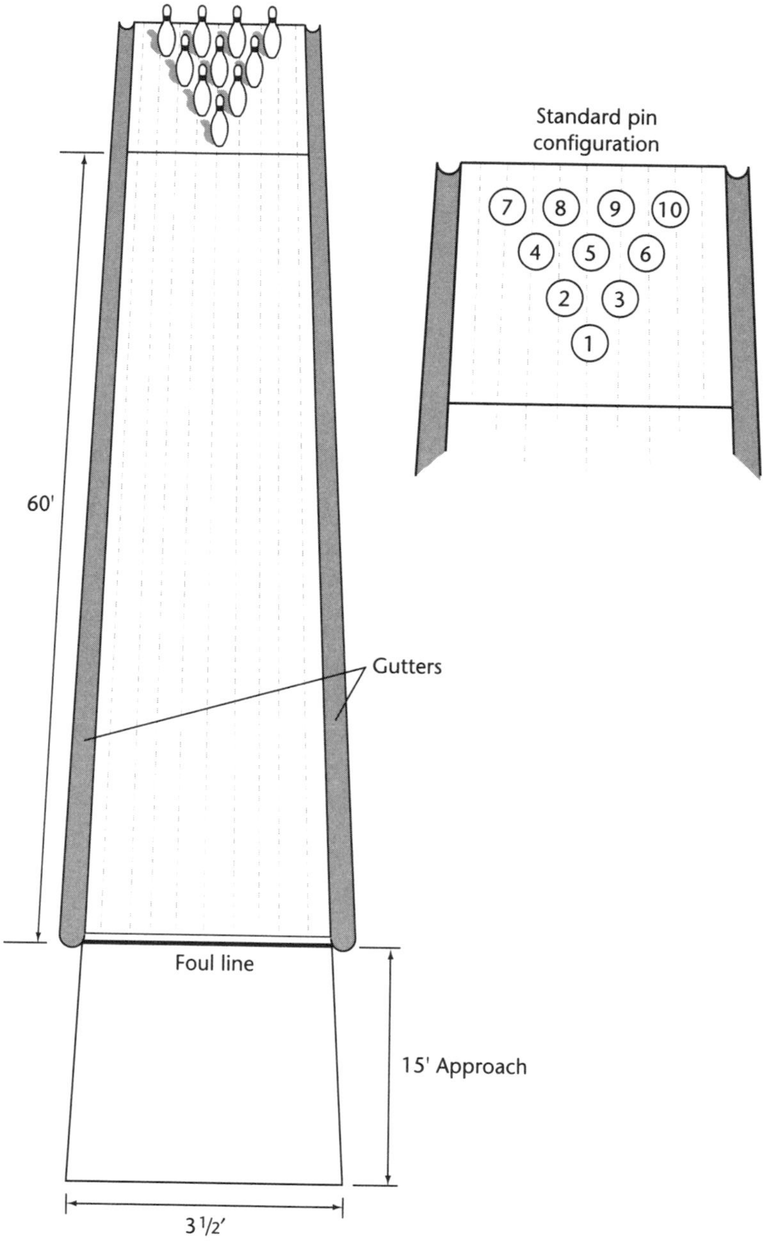

Figure 34. A regulation bowling lane, made of maple and pine wood or a simulated-wood veneer, is 3½ feet wide and measures 60 feet from the foul line to the headpin; it takes about two and a half seconds for a pro's ball to reach the pins. The various pins are always referenced by standardized numbering, 1 to 10 (i.e., the middle pin is the 5, the left rear pin is the 7, etc.).

Suspenseful Scoring

The essence of bowling's drama springs from its unique scoring system, which rewards excellent shots with chances for bonus points. To win the top tournaments, players must earn virtually all of these bonus opportunities and convert them into extra points.

Here is how the scoring system works:

For each frame, a player is given up to two chances to bowl the ball and knock down the 10 pins. If he knocks down all 10 with the first ball, that is called a "strike" and is worth at least 10 points; for bowling a strike, he is entitled to add to that frame's total whatever points he scores with the next two balls. Therefore, the best possible score for one frame is 30; a perfect game is 300, or 10 perfect frames. (A perfect game is a rarity. Throughout an entire pro tournament, only three to five perfect games will be bowled among all competitors.)

If all 10 pins have been knocked down after the second ball of a frame, that is called a "spare," and the bowler earns the chance to add whatever points he scores with the next ball. If, for example, eight pins are toppled with the next ball, the total for the frame with the spare is 18 (10 + 8).

As an illustration, here's a sample scorecard for one game:

Frame 1	Frame 2	Frame 3	Frame 4	Frame 5	Frame 6	Frame 7	Frame 8	Frame 9	Frame 10
X	X	X	7 2	8 /	9 –	X	5 /	9 –	X X 8
30	**57**	**76**	**85**	**104**	**113**	**133**	**152**	**161**	**189**

Figure 35. The scorecard encapsulates the bowler's performance throughout a game, frame by frame. Bowling's unique scoring system provides for bonus points and competitive drama.

In the first frame, the bowler throws a strike with the first ball (signified by an "X" in the small box at the upper left). That gives him at least 10 points in the first frame, plus a bonus for the number of pins he knocks down with the next two balls.

In the second frame, he bowls another strike, and an "X" is marked in that frame. (There is still no complete score for the first or second frame.)

In frame three, he bowls another strike. With that ball, he has bowled twice since the first strike, completing the two bonus balls earned from the first strike. Therefore, a total of 30 points can be entered for the first frame.

In frame four, he knocks down seven pins with the first ball (completing the two bonus balls from his second strike) and two with his second ball (completing the two bonus balls from his third strike). Therefore, a total of 27 points has been earned for the second frame for a cumulative total of 57, and 19 points for the third frame for a cumulative total of 76 points.

Since no bonus balls were earned in the fourth frame, that total can be tallied, too—9 points, for a running total of 85.

Beginning frame five, he knocks down eight pins with the first ball and the remaining two with the second ball for a spare (signified by a diagonal line through the second small box), which gives him one bonus ball.

In the sixth frame, he knocks down nine pins (completing the previous frame's score of 19 for a running total of 104) and misses the remaining pin with the second ball (signified with a horizontal line in the small box in the upper right). Therefore, he gains 9 points in frame six for a cumulative score of 113.

In frame seven, he throws a strike.

In frame eight, he knocks down five pins with the first ball and converts the spare with the second (completing the two bonus balls for the strike in frame seven. Twenty points are gained in frame seven for a running total of 133).

In frame nine, the pinfall is nine for the first delivery (completing frame eight with 19 points for a cumulative total of 152) and none for the second. Running total through frame nine is 161.

In the tenth and final frame, he bowls a strike, earning two bonus balls. With the first he throws another strike and with the second knocks down eight pins for a total of 28 points. Final total is 189.

How the Pros Play It

Pros shoot for strikes and only grudgingly settle for spares. An unconverted spare (called an "open frame") is despised because only strikes and spares earn those vitally important bonus balls for extra points.

Unless luck intervenes, a strike is always made in one specific way (see Figure 36): the ball must curve in from the right (for right-handed bowlers), simultaneously hitting the 1 and 3 pins (called the "1-3 pocket") on its way toward hitting the 5 and 9 pins. The other pins will be toppled by pins, not by the ball. Here is the sought-after chain reaction for a strike: the 5 pin takes out the 8, and the 3 takes the 6, which takes the 10; meanwhile, the 1 hits the 2, the 2 gets the 4, and the 4 topples the 7.

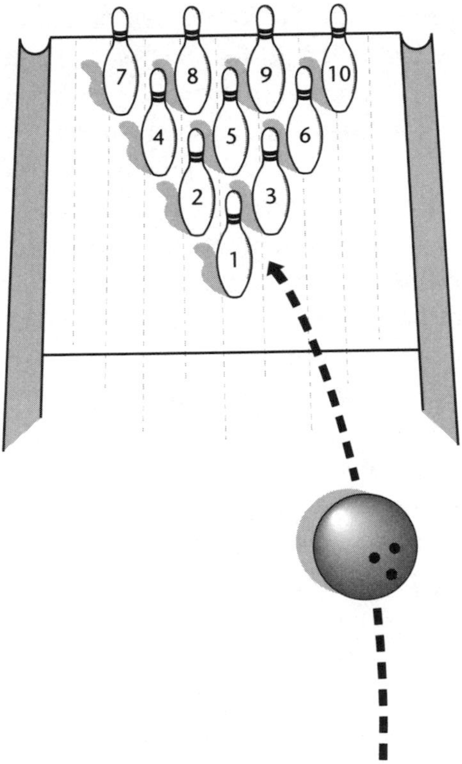

Figure 36. A player's primary objective is to bowl a strike—to knock down all 10 pins with the first ball. To do so, the ball must curve in (called a "hook") and hit four specific pins: the 1, 3, 5, and 9. The remaining six pins will topple as they are struck by falling pins. (For a left-hander, the ball hooks from the other side to hit the 1, 2, 5, and 8.)

Troubles come when the strike is missed and the bowler must face a "spare leave." Leaves come in a variety of formations, requiring the bowler to draw upon a variety of shots—some very difficult to execute—in order to convert the spare. The seven most difficult leaves are the 7-10, 4-6, 4-6-7-10, 4-6-7, 6-7-10, 4-6-7-9-10, and 4-6-7-8-10 (see Figure 37). The first three are the most dreaded of all and require "help-from-above" to convert. (Incidentally, the pin most commonly left standing after the first delivery is the 10—sometimes called a "ringing 10" when still standing after a seemingly perfect shot.)

The ideal throw for a strike will do a skid-roll-hook pattern, meaning that the ball will skid for the first few yards along the oiled surface of the lane, then begin to roll. If thrown with the proper amount of lift and momentum, about 15 feet from the pins the ball will begin to curve in sharply (or "hook") toward the 1-3 pocket.

"Lift" is defined as the extra forward momentum imparted to a ball as it is released. This is achieved with the two middle fingers as they slide out of the grip holes and by proper follow-through of the bowler's arm motion. Lift will cause the ball to plow through the pins with more power and better results because the ball will skid less and roll (revolve, or "rev") more. The average bowler's ball will complete 8 to 12 rotations down the lane; a pro's ball will make 14 to 18 revs. Higher revs usually translate into more force and better pinfalls.

Complicating the bowler's task, lane conditions vary significantly with humidity and temperature and especially with how the lane is "dressed" (that is, how the lane oil has been applied prior to play). By carefully observing how the ball moves down the lane during the practice session and as the game progresses, the player must figure out how and where the lane has been oiled. Oil greatly affects the ball's behavior as well as the bowler's ability to control it.

Usually, the first 35 to 45 feet of lane are covered with a thin coat of oil, sometimes thicker toward the edges or middle and sometimes laid down in a Christmas-tree pattern. Once past the oiled portion of the lane, the ball will grip the surface better, enabling it to react more responsively to whatever "English," or spin on the ball, has been imparted by the bowler.

In pro tournaments, the lanes tend to be exceedingly well dressed and, as a result, are unusually difficult to read and more challenging.

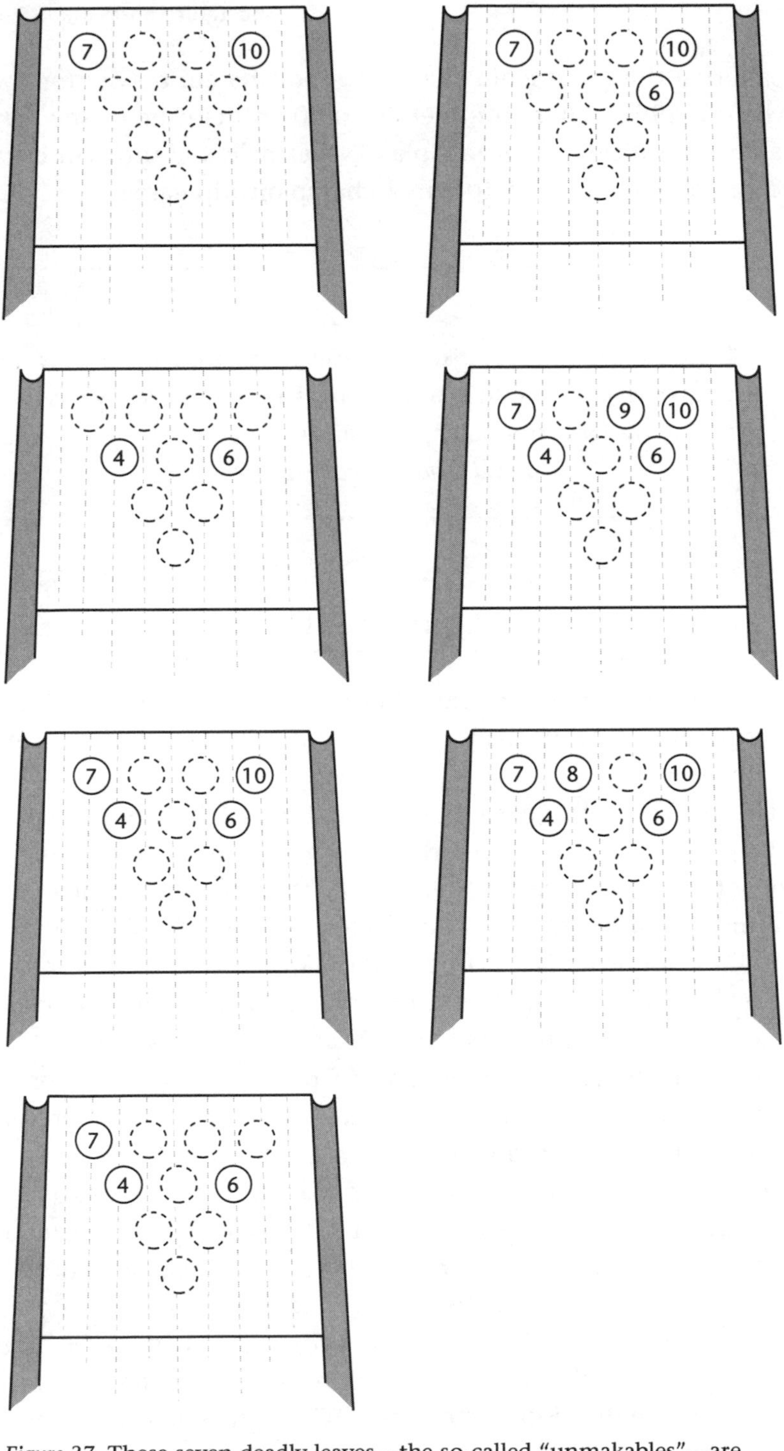

Figure 37. These seven deadly leaves—the so-called "unmakables"—are considered the most difficult in bowling and are rarely converted to spares.

It's said that the game score of a very good amateur bowler (one who bowls, say, 190) would plummet 30 to 40 points if he or she played on a lane conditioned for pro play. Nevertheless, a pro will usually need to score at least 235 to win a championship game.

"There are two types of strikes in bowling: excellent shots and the lucky variety. I define an excellent shot as a strike thrown by me. The lucky strike is any thrown by my opponent."

—David Ozio, champion bowler

Equipment

Before every tournament, the lanes, pins, and players' equipment are scrutinized by officials to make certain they meet standardized specifications.

The ball, which measures eight and a half inches in diameter (slightly smaller than a basketball), is made of reactive resin, urethane, or plastic and cannot weigh more than 16 pounds (among the pros, men usually use a 16-pound ball; women sometimes use one around 15 pounds). Three finger holes are custom drilled into the ball so the athlete's thumb and two middle fingers can comfortably grip it for delivery. A top-caliber ball can cost up to $300.

At tournaments, a pro may have 15 to 25 balls on hand for various shots and changing climatic conditions. For straight, precision shots to convert spares, a plastic ball is often used. To shoot powerful, high-rev balls that hook well for strikes, a reactive resin or a urethane ball is used. The reactive resin ball (basically a urethane ball with a plasticizer additive) is the most technologically advanced ball and preferred by most pros for a powerful strike ball.

Shoes are soft and pliable; a pair costs about $150. For right-handed bowlers, the sole for the left shoe is made of smooth leather to facilitate sliding at delivery. The right sole is made of rubber for traction.

The lane, measuring 60 feet from the foul line to the headpin (or king pin) and 3½ feet wide, has traditionally been made of maple and pine boards running lengthwise. The lane is perfectly level and coated with polyurethane and an oil finish. A regulation lane is 39 boards wide; most accomplished bowlers use specific boards to help them aim various shots.

In recent years, most new lanes and practically all lanes used by pros are made of synthetic, Formica-like materials. These simulated-wood lanes are still oiled as real-wood lanes are, but they are more durable, require less maintenance, and provide a more consistent playing surface.

A pin—standing 15 inches high, weighing about 3½ pounds and measuring 4¾ inches at its thickest point—is built for punishment and durability. When struck by the ball (traveling about 17 mph), the pin must withstand an impact of about 2,000 pounds per square inch and, when struck by another pin, about 1,200 pounds per square inch. It is made of 19 pieces of pressure-laminated maple; the wooden billet is then shaped on a lathe, covered with a nylon sleeve (or "sock"), and protected with several coats of plastic gel. As finishing touches, the neck stripes are painted on and decals applied.

Life in the Pro Lane

Most professional male bowlers are members of the Professional Bowlers Association (PBA), established in 1958 and headquartered in Akron, Ohio. Nationally, there are seven PBA regions in which about 3,000 of its members compete. To qualify for PBA membership, a bowler must maintain an average score of 200 for at least 66 games a year for two consecutive years.

About 100 of the very best pros join the PBA Tour and challenge each other in about 26 four-day tournaments a year, many televised, from late January through November. The pro tour culminates with the annual Tournament of Champions, the sport's most prestigious event. Top players on the tour win about $200,000 to $300,000 in prize money a year, plus product-endorsement and appearance fees. Touring pros range in age from about 20 to 55.

The PBA Tour's traveling entourage includes an on-the-road support staff of 10 and two tractor trailers loaded with several hundred balls, two ball-drilling machines, shoes and other equipment, plus a mobile pressroom and office. The tour also includes an advance team of two to three lane-maintenance specialists.

The Professional Women's Bowling Association (PWBA), founded in 1981, includes about 250 players at the regional level and 40 touring pros, ranging in age from about 20 to 40. The pro tour holds 22 three-day tournaments a year, scheduled from February through November, with a televised championship that concludes the season.

At such rarefied levels of play, the best pro bowlers have very strong powers of concentration. Absolute focus is necessary to deliver the ball with unerring precision and perfect timing, again and again throughout a demanding tournament.

To keep physically fit, bowlers often work out with light weights to strengthen and condition their shoulders and arms and jog to keep their legs in shape. Because a smooth, balanced delivery depends upon flexed knees, the rigors of a four-day tournament can catch up with a player who's not physically fit, especially in the legs.

Other Important Stuff

Deflection: When a ball hits a pin, the impact will edge the ball off its previous course or line. This is called deflection and can ruin an intended shot if the bowler has failed to account for it accurately in his delivery. To overcome excessive deflection, most top bowlers use a reactive-resin ball for its gripping ability and deliver the ball with momentum and lift.

Gutter ball: The trough on both sides and running the length of the lane is called the gutter. A poorly thrown ball that rolls into the trough is called a gutter ball and will not hit any pins.

Pin action: How active the pins become once they are struck by the ball and topple, hopefully hitting nearby pins and causing them to fall, too. For a strike, the ball usually hits only four pins; pin action brings down the other six.

Split: Combinations of pins left standing after the first delivery where at least one pin space separates the standing pins; the headpin must be down, too. A split is usually a difficult leave to convert to a spare because of deflection and tricky angles. Pin combinations such as 2-8 or 5-10 are especially challenging splits.

History

Various forms of bowling have been played around the world since ancient times. In the 1890s, an English archeologist discovered an Egyptian tomb that contained miniature pins and a ball made of stone dating to about 3200 B.C. The ancient Polynesians played a pin-and-ball game called "ula maika." King Henry VIII built one of the first indoor bowling courts for lawn bowling. As the Spanish Armada approached England in 1588, Sir Francis Drake is said to have lawn bowled while waiting for the tide to change so his ships could attack.

The modern game of tenpins is a direct descendent of a European game called "ninepins," which early settlers brought to the New World. At Jamestown, Virginia, England's first permanent settlement in America, the leadership groused that the playing of ninepins was sapping too much time and energy from the struggling enterprise. In 1611, one newly arrived dignitary upbraided the settlers for "bowling in the streets" instead of "repairing their houses ready to fall on their heads."

"Nothing interrupted the stillness of the scene but the noise of the [ninepin] balls, which, whenever they were rolled, echoed along the mountains like rumbling peals of thunder."

—Washington Irving, "Rip Van Winkle," 1820

Among America's rich and famous of the late nineteenth and early twentieth centuries, it was fashionable to install a private bowling alley in one's mansion. The grand homes of the Rockefellers, Vanderbilts, Astors, Goulds, and others provided tenpin bowling lanes for entertainment of their guests.

In more recent times, tenpins has challenged the talents of baseball great Babe Ruth, comedian Jerry Lewis, and presidents Richard Nixon and Bill Clinton.

According to the American Bowling Congress (ABC), founded in New York City in 1895 to standardize tenpins' rules and equipment, about 10 million Americans compete regularly in league play sanctioned by either the ABC or the WIBC (Women's International Bowling Congress, organized in 1916).

Worldwide, it is estimated that about 100 million people in 100 countries bowl tenpins regularly; in recent years its popularity has risen dramatically in Asian countries. The Federation Internationale des Quilleurs, established in 1951, oversees the sport around the globe and enforces standardized play.

chapter seven

GOLF

"The man who has never stood upon the tee with a keen rival near him and driven a perfect ball, the hands having followed well through and finished nicely up against the head, while the little white speck in the distance, after skimming the earth for a time, rises and soars upwards, clearing all obstacles, and seeming to revel in its freedom and speed until at last it dips gracefully back to the turf again—I say that the man who has not done this has missed one of the joys of life."

—*Harry Vardon,* The Complete Golfer, *1905*

The Basics

Professional golf is a succession of shrewd, calculated assessments and masterful shotmaking—all occurring in an idealized setting of verdant woodlands and meadowlands, babbling brooks, and mirror-like ponds. This pristinely landscaped tract of real estate (called the "course") usually covers 150 to 200 acres. With the possible exception of alpine skiing, no other sport matches golf's playing areas for aesthetic appeal.

"Give me golf clubs, the fresh air, and a beautiful partner, and you can keep the golf clubs and the fresh air."

—*Jack Benny, comedian*

A golf course consists of 18 long playing areas called "holes." Each hole is numbered and must be played in sequence. On average, a hole is about 380 yards long (see Figure 38), but length varies significantly. Width varies, too, with fairways averaging about 40 yards wide.

At one end of each hole is an initial hitting area called the "tee"; at the other end is a carefully manicured plot called the "putting green." Strategically located on each green is a small hole or "cup" (4.25 inches in diameter and 4 inches deep). Between the tee and green is a long expanse of mowed grass called the "fairway." Situated diabolically along the fairway and around the green are trouble spots called "hazards"—pits of sand called "bunkers," ponds and streams, as well as obstacles such as groves of trees and tall grass (called "the rough"). Hazards and obstacles are designed to challenge a golfer's nerve, test his judgment and shotmaking abilities, and punish his mistakes.

To conquer the course, each golfer is equipped with a hard, white ball (1.68 inches in diameter) and a set of not more than 14 long-shafted clubs for hitting various shots. The object of the game is to hit the golf ball from the tee down the fairway and eventually into the cup. Throughout the entire course, the player who accomplishes this with the least number of hits, or "strokes," is the victor. (Each player is responsible for keeping track of his or her score, hole by hole, on an official scorecard. An inaccurate tally at the end of a tournament can automatically disqualify that player.)

Each hole presents distinctive challenges. Some are long (around 580 yards); others are short (about 150 yards). Some fairways are broad, others narrow. Some are bordered by thick stands of trees, others by tall grass. Some fairways are straight; others bend to the left or right (called "doglegs"). Some are made more treacherous by water hazards (ponds or streams). Most are complicated by bunkers (some-

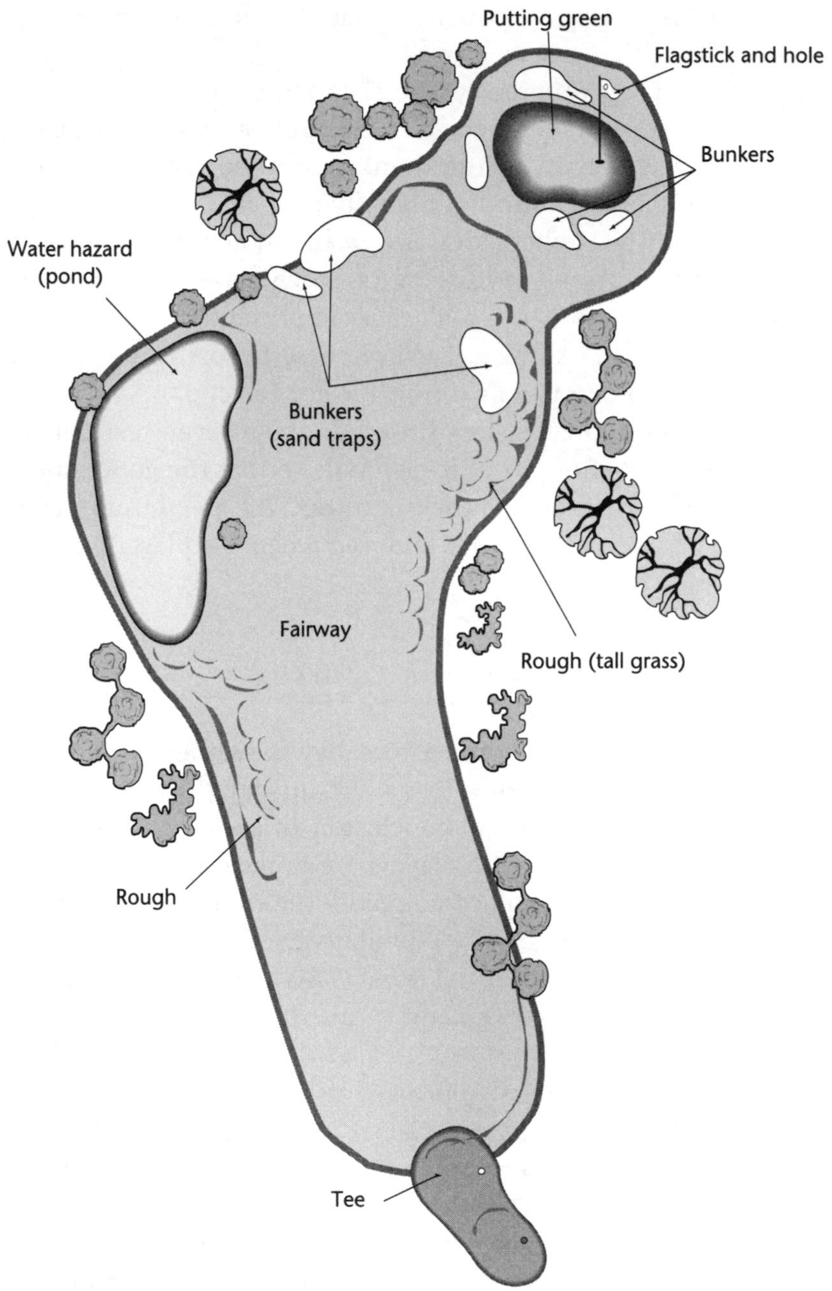

Figure 38. A typical fairway is about 380 yards long. To make it more challenging to the golfer, bunkers (sand traps) and water hazards (streams and ponds) are often added. In most cases, trees and "the rough" (tall grass) threaten along the edges. In this example, the fairway bends (or "doglegs") to the right.

times called "sand traps"), usually situated next to the green and sometimes along the fairway as well.

Each green plays differently, too. The most obvious differences are where the actual hole is located (tucked into a tight corner, along a perilous slope, near a yawning bunker or pond) and the green's physical shape (oblong, round, kidney-shaped, etc.).

The accomplished golfer assesses a green's more subtle variations, too, such as the type and texture of its closely mowed grass, which way the blades tend to bend, and, most importantly, the slope and contour of the green's surface. Each of these factors can affect the pace and direction of a ball as it rolls toward the cup.

There's a removable flagstick (it stands about seven feet tall and is sometimes called the "pin") in each hole so that the golfer knows where the hole is when he hits the ball toward the green from the tee or fairway. The flagstick must be removed when the player putts for the cup.

Par for the Course

In most pro tournaments, competitors play the same 18 holes four times during a four-day period (usually Thursday through Sunday) for a total of 72 holes. At the conclusion of each set of 18 holes (called a "round of golf"), the players are ranked according to the number of strokes each took to complete the round. At the end of four days and four rounds, the cumulative scores are tallied, and the player with the lowest total wins. This is the most common method of tournament scoring and is called either "stroke play" or "medal play."

In the case of a tie, most tournaments are settled by a "sudden death" play-off, whereby the tied players play another hole; whoever wins that hole wins the tournament. In the case of a continuing tie, additional holes are played until one player prevails.

In addition to cumulative totals, scores are always related to "par," which is the predetermined number of strokes that an expert player theoretically should take to play a specific hole or round. Each hole carries a designated "par," as does the entire 18 holes for each golf course. Par for all tournament holes is three, four, or five. Generally, par-3 holes are less than 250 yards, par 4s are 251 to 470, and par 5s are over 470.

As an example, for a par-4 hole, an expert player should hit the ball into the cup ("sink the putt") with his fourth stroke ("be down in four"). His first shot will be hit off the tee and fly down the fairway about 250 to 280 yards. His second shot of about 120 to 150 yards should land on the green. With two more strokes, he should putt the ball into the cup to "make par" on that hole. If he should hole the ball in three strokes instead of four, that would be one stroke under par and is called a "birdie." If he should sink the ball in two strokes under par, that's called an "eagle" and is relatively rare. Holing the ball in one stroke over par is a "bogey"; two strokes over par is a "double bogey."

In 1899, so the story goes, a man named George Crump was playing at The Country Club of Atlantic City when his ball struck a bird in midair. Nevertheless, he managed to play the hole in one under par, prompting one of his golfing partners to dub his feat a "birdie."

Par for a full round (18 holes) is usually 72 (sometimes 70 or 71) for most regulation courses, and therefore 288 for an entire four-round tournament. In addition to posting the running total for each player on the tournament's scoreboard (often called the "leaderboard"), a player's score is also displayed in relation to par. For example, if a player's cumulative score is 140 after completing two rounds on a par-72 course, he is said to have played four under par (par for two rounds would be 144). The leaderboard would display his last name (listed in rank order), followed by his total score for each of the first two rounds (for example, 69 and 71), and his cumulative score of 140, followed by a –4 (indicating four strokes under par).

"Match play" is another form of competition whereby the score is determined by the number of holes won, rather than the cumulative number of strokes in "stroke play." In match play, a winner is determined when a player leads in the number of holes won by more than the number of holes remaining to be played. The U.S. Amateur tournament uses match play.

Basic Rules

The fundamental rule of golf is "Play the ball as it lies." With a few technical exceptions, only a club may touch the ball from the time it's hit from the tee until it's putted into the hole. The ball must be hit from wherever it lands on the fairway or the green—including from tall grass, bunkers, behind trees, etc.

If the ball's circumstance (or "lie") is deemed unplayable, then that player is penalized by one extra stroke being added to his score; he must then hit a new ball from immediately near the unplayable ball. If he hits into an unplayably deep water hazard, then he is penalized a stroke and must hit another ball from the shoreline where the lost ball last crossed over the water or from where he hit the last shot.

If a player hits a ball that he subsequently can't find, or if he hits a wild shot that veers so far off the fairway that it goes out-of-bounds, then he is penalized a stroke and must hit another ball from where he made the last shot.

Club Selection

Of the 14 golf clubs that a player is allowed to carry in a tournament, each is designed and precisely made for hitting specific shots. Most top golfers are proficient with all of them.

There are two basic types of clubs (see Figure 39)—"woods" and "irons." Woods have larger, rounded clubheads and longer shafts and are used primarily for hitting long-distance shots. The clubheads for irons are flat and rectangular; they are used mostly for shorter shots that demand a higher degree of accuracy. Until about 15 years ago, the terms "woods" and "irons" could be used almost literally. The clubheads of practically all woods were actually made of wood (the best were made of persimmon), and irons were made of steel. Because of recent metallurgic advances to improve hitting performance, the best clubheads are now made of pricey high-tech metals like titanium and beryllium.

Both types of club are classified by a number, each according to its "loft," that is, the degree of tilt designed into the clubhead's strik-

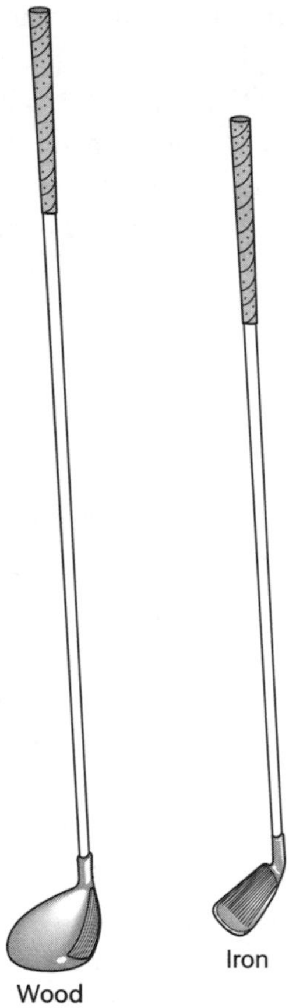

Figure 39. The two basic types of golf clubs are woods (for long-distance shots) and irons (for shorter shots requiring more accuracy). The shafts of woods are longer for added power and distance.

ing surface. A 1-wood or a 1-iron, for example, has practically no loft. Each is used for low, long shots that usually gain extra yardage by rolling. A 5-wood or a 5-iron, however, has significantly more loft. The ball travels in a higher arc and doesn't roll as far.

The degree of loft (and the way the player swings the club) has another effect on the ball: it dictates the ball's spin when airborne. At the advanced level of play, spin provides a critical difference in a ball's distance and direction as well as the player's control of it once the ball hits the ground. The higher the degree of loft, the more the clubface will impart backspin to the ball when hit. The more backspin imparted to a ball, the less it will bounce and roll when it hits the ground. This helps the player control the ball and place it where he or she wants it. As an example, for an approach shot to the green, a player might use a 9-iron, imparting a high arc and plenty of backspin to the ball. The ball will drop soundly onto the green and stop close to where it landed.

The 14 clubs that a pro selects to carry during a tournament are chosen to complement that player's individual style of play. A pro's golf bag might contain a 1-wood (called a "driver"), a 3-wood, irons 2 through 9, a lob wedge, a sand wedge, a pitching wedge, and a putter. The three wedges (which are also irons) have the highest degree of loft and are used for finesse shots to the green or to hit out of bunkers. The putter is used to gently hit (or "putt") the ball so that it rolls across the green toward the cup.

Course Strategy: The Winning Ingredient

All touring pros are accomplished shot-makers, but very few consistently win big tournaments. The game's standouts—exemplified by Ben Hogan in the 1940s and '50s and Jack Nicklaus in the 1960s, '70s, and '80s—not only match or exceed their opponents' shotmaking abilities, they play the course smarter.

In addition to mastering the mechanics of a successful golf swing, the top pros learn to carefully analyze the key aspects of each course and hole they play, then mastermind a strategy for conquest. Assessing each situation more shrewdly and comprehensively than most players, they know when to take risks and when to play it safe. They also have a keen appreciation for their own shotmaking strengths and limitations, and they factor those into their deliberations.

Strategic factors often include the course's overall length—does it favor a long game (strong wood shots) or a short game (finesse shots with irons)? Do the fairways favor players with a good "draw" (shots with a controlled curve to the left, for right-handers) or a good "fade" (shots with a controlled curve to the right)? Are strong winds predicted during the tournament? If so, how strong and from which direction? What about rain? (Wetness has significant club-selection implications because it's much harder to impart spin to a ball that's lying in wet grass; less spin means less control.)

Generally, the best golfers play aggressively but avoid undue risks. They are intent upon making birdies, not eagles. They'll settle for par on most holes and even an occasional bogey. A pro will press harder for birdies on par-5 holes, usually by attempting to make the green on the second shot instead of the third, particularly if his drive was aggressively long and placed the ball in good position on the fairway.

Once on the green, a player usually plans for two putting attempts to sink the ball.

To make par on a par-5 hole, it's generally assumed that a player makes a good drive from the tee, followed by a strong shot from the fairway to just short of the green, followed by a short "chip shot" onto the green, followed by two putts. A par score always assumes two putts to sink the ball. So for a par-3 hole, the player's tee shot should land on the green (see Figure 40).

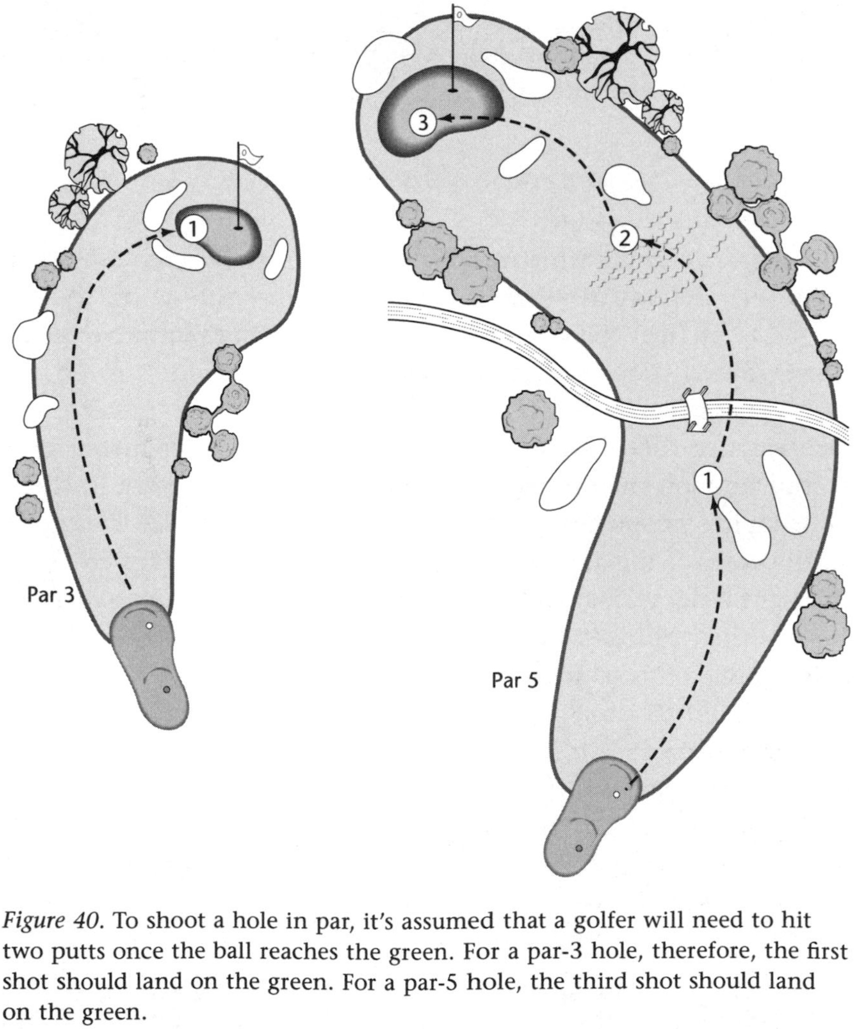

Figure 40. To shoot a hole in par, it's assumed that a golfer will need to hit two putts once the ball reaches the green. For a par-3 hole, therefore, the first shot should land on the green. For a par-5 hole, the third shot should land on the green.

The Caddie's Role

The pro golfer plays with an assistant called a "caddie," whose primary job is to carry the player's bag of clubs and offer advice on club selection, based primarily on estimated distances from the holes as well as the player's shotmaking abilities. Good caddies also offer pertinent observations about weather and course conditions. During play, the caddie is the only person from whom the player may solicit advice.

In the best player/caddie relationships, the caddie also provides psychological support by providing positive comments and encouragement to the player.

Generally, the caddie is paid a salary plus up to 10 percent of a player's tournament earnings.

Practice and Training

Pro golfers are good athletes with excellent hand-eye coordination and sense of body rhythm for smooth, powerful swings. Some, referred to as "feel" players, hit the ball with a more intuitive swing. Others take a more cognitive approach by concentrating on the mechanics of the swing. As a loose generalization, the former spend more practice time playing on a golf course; the latter invest more practice time on the driving range with a coach, or "swing teacher," and studying videotapes of themselves hitting the ball (see Figure 41).

To stay in shape, most work with a fitness trainer. Many work out with light weights, jog, and—most importantly—maintain a regimen of stretching exercises to keep their swings loose and fluid and to avoid muscle pulls or strains.

"Golf is a good walk spoiled."
—*Mark Twain*

Most pros spend much time practicing on or near the greens (called the "short game"). In a tournament, the majority of shots

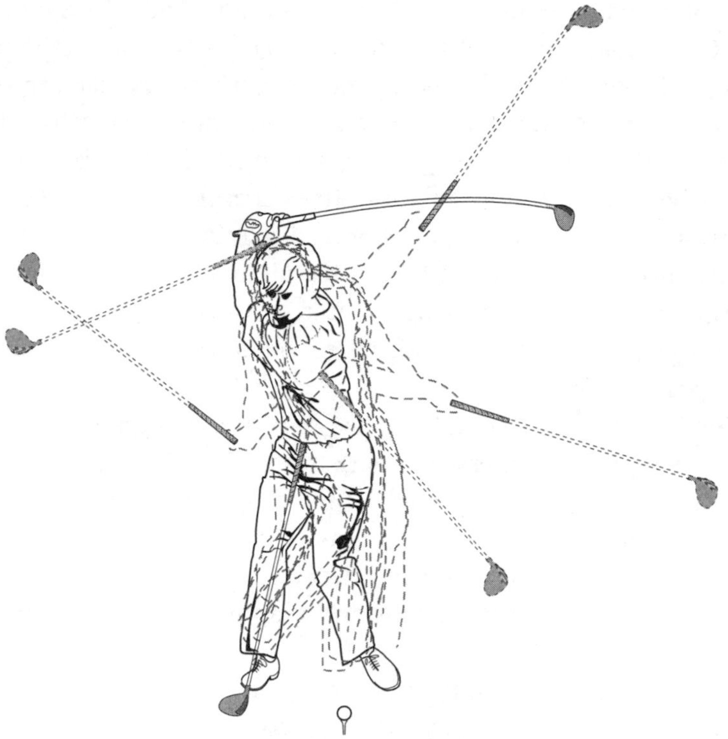

Figure 41. A golf swing's power comes from the large muscles of the torso. The torso twists in the backswing and releases tremendous torque as it unwinds in the forward swing. The explosive power of Tiger Woods's famous swing, for example, is generated by this forceful unwinding, measured to be 20 to 50 percent faster than that of other golfers on the pro tour.

they must hit are short "approach" shots to the green and putts—both of which require fine-tuned finesse and accuracy. Many closely contested matches have been captured by superior chipping and putting.

Equipment

Over the past two decades, technological advances in club design and construction materials have significantly improved the performance of both woods and irons.

Strong, lightweight metals like titanium provide for a more consistent clubhead construction and a larger "sweet spot" (the perfect place on the clubface for striking the ball), which translate into more reliable shots, greater distances, and more confident swings by the player. Some clubheads for irons are still made of steel, but many are now made of beryllium and sometimes titanium with nickel, brass, or tungsten inserts for proper weight distribution.

Like modern-day alchemists, golf club manufacturers continue to experiment with new space-age materials in their competitive quest for stronger, lighter metallic alloys to create the ultimate shafts and clubheads.

The best clubs carry hefty price tags (the top golfers, of course, are given their equipment by marketing-minded manufacturers). A top-of-the-line set of irons (eight clubs) costs about $750 to $2,000, the less-expensive sets being of stainless steel, the pricier constructed with titanium heads. Top-of-the-line woods cost $200 to $600 each—those made with titanium heads and graphite shafts being the most expensive.

Although golf balls have also experienced design and construction revisions in recent years (larger cores for distance and more durable covers) with increased distance the main objective, most touring pros still prefer the "feel" and control of a traditionally constructed ball—consisting of a central core tightly wrapped with a very long strand of rubber and covered with a tough but pliable outer material called balata. All balls have a dimpled surface for distance and control (see Figure 42).

Figure 42. Why are golf balls dimpled? A dimpled ball can be hit much farther than a smooth one, according to tests by the U.S. Golf Association. Remarkably, a smooth ball hit 120 yards would have traveled 260 yards if dimpled. The dimples substantially reduce air resistance.

Major Tournaments

Most televised golf tournaments are sanctioned by the Professional Golfers Association (PGA) or the Ladies Professional Golf Association (LPGA). Both the U.S. Open and the U.S. Women's Open are sponsored by the U.S. Golf Association (USGA), an organization started in 1894 to oversee and promote the sport.

In men's pro golf, the annual "big four" tournaments are the Masters (Augusta, Georgia), the U.S. Open (course locations vary), the British Open (rotates among courses in England and Scotland), and the PGA Championship (course locations vary). Another significant event is the Ryder Cup, a biennial competition between teams from Europe and the United States (unlike most other tournaments, it's based upon match play).

The Senior PGA Tour, organized in 1980 and featuring pros over 50 years old, includes the PGA Seniors' Championship and the U.S. Senior Open.

On the women's pro circuit, the majors are the Nabisco Dinah Shore, the LPGA Championship, the U.S. Women's Open, and the du Maurier Classic (in Ontario). The Solheim Cup pits teams from the United States and Europe in match play.

Other Important Stuff

Club pro: At most public or private golf courses the club pro is responsible for the daily operation of the course and equipment shop, as well as for providing golf lessons for customers. All have distinguished themselves as golf players.

Divot: A small chunk of turf knocked out of the ground by the clubhead (usually an iron) when striking the ball. Etiquette requires that it be replaced by the caddie or player.

Hook: To hit the ball so that it curves significantly from right to left (for a right-handed player). A slight, controlled hook is called a "draw."

Slice: To hit the ball so that it curves significantly from left to right (for a right-handed player). A slight, controlled slice is called a "fade."

Tee: A small, wooden peg which holds the ball about an inch above the ground and can be used only on "tee" shots—the initial shot for each hole. (An American dentist named William Lowell is credited with inventing the wooden tee in 1920 and launched The Reddy Tee Co.)

History

Golf's heritage follows a pastoral trail back to its roots in Scotland, still considered mecca by all serious players and fans of the game. There are written records about golf (early spellings include "goff" and "gowf") as early as 1457, when James II of Scotland denounced the game as detracting from archery, an important pursuit for the defense of the country. Apparently, golf was already well established by that time.

During its formative era in Scotland, golf was played in open grasslands along the seashore. These areas, called "links," are treeless, windswept stretches of flat terrain and rolling sand dunes covered with short, wild grasses. Even today, the oldest and most famous courses of Scotland and Ireland retain that appearance and heritage. On most golf courses throughout the world, the bunker—or sand trap—is a vestige of the Scottish links courses.

Early on, the game caught the eye of royalty. Mary, Queen of Scots, played golf in the 1560s. By 1604, records show that James I of England (formally James VI of Scotland) had retained a royal clubmaker. In those days, makers of archery bows and fishing rods were sometimes hired to craft golf clubs because they understood the flexible properties of various woods. Blacksmiths made the irons.

The earliest clubs were fashioned from one piece of wood. Those were superseded by clubheads crafted from a single block of wood, then spliced to the shaft, which was usually made of ash and later hickory. Grips were made of sheepskin.

As early as 1743, shipping bills of lading show that clubs and balls were being exported from Scotland to the American colonies, specifically Virginia and South Carolina, and soon thereafter to Maryland.

In 1744, the Company of Gentlemen Golfers met in Leith, Scotland, to establish a club and set down written rules. A decade later, a group at nearby St. Andrews organized a golf competition with a silver-club trophy. This group became the Royal & Ancient Club of St. Andrews and drew up its own set of rules, which formed the basis for those in effect today. The St. Andrews course eventually evolved into the first with 18 holes. The Royal & Ancient is still considered the foremost and most prestigious golf organization in the world and, together with the U.S. Golf Association which formed in 1894, oversees and regulates the sport throughout most of the world.

Early golf balls were made with a bull-hide cover jam-packed with boiled breast feathers from chickens or geese (more feathers than could be held in a man's top hat were compressed into one of these leather balls, about the same size as a modern golf ball). Back then, a ball—called a "feathery"—cost two to three times more than a club. Golf was a game only for the prosperous few.

As Britain's commercial and military presence expanded throughout the nineteenth century, British and Scottish businessmen became golf's apostles by spreading the game to foreign lands. Golf clubs were established in Calcutta in 1830, Bombay in 1842, and Montreal in 1873.

The sport's popularity accelerated in the mid-1800s with the introduction of the gutta-percha ball (known as the "gutty"), a much cheaper ball made from the sap of a Malaysian tree. By the turn of the century, the gutty was being replaced by a more advanced ball developed in Akron, Ohio. This new ball featured a central core tightly wrapped with a long strand of rubber and covered with a tough coat of gutta-percha (replaced soon after by balata gum). Golf balls have changed little since then.

Mechanical mowing machines also helped spread the game by enabling courses to be built and maintained on inland meadowlands, where without mowing, the grasses grew too high for golf.

As the sport matured and became more organized, so did interest in competitive forums. Although the first stroke-play tournament was held at St. Andrews in the mid-1700s, it was not until a century later, in 1860, that the first British Open was held. The U.S. Open dates back to 1895; the PGA championship began in 1916; the first Masters was held in 1934; and the Ryder Cup began in 1927. In women's golf, the U.S. Women's Open dates back to 1946; the LPGA championship began in 1955; the Nabisco Dinah Shore tournament started in 1972; and the first du Maurier Classic was held in 1973.

In the United States, the first course with a custom-built clubhouse was constructed in 1891 at Shinnecock Hills, New York. Indicative of the sport's snowballing popularity, by 1900 there were 26 golf clubs in the Chicago area alone.

About this time, the sport's first luminaries of the twentieth century began to appear. The great British golfer Harry Vardon made a hugely successful tour of the United States in 1901. (It's said that when he played a course near New York City, the stock exchange closed for the day.) Bobby Jones, Walter Hagen, Gene Sarazen, and others attracted even more visibility and excitement to the game in the '20s and '30s.

Then, over the next 30 years, came a whole stream of electrifying champions, notably Byron Nelson, Ben Hogan, Sam Snead, Arnold Palmer, and Jack Nicklaus (the only player to win each of the four major tournaments at least three times and perhaps the greatest golfer of all time). Among women golfers during this explosive period, the brightest stars were "Babe" Didrikson Zaharias, Louise Suggs, Betsy Rawls, Mickey Wright, and Kathy Whitworth.

In the 1980s and 1990s, golf's unprecedented growth in popularity and television revenues sent prize money soaring on both the men's and women's tours. PGA tournament purses have almost tripled in the past decade. Among the top 10 money winners on the tour, annual prize money averages $1.7 million. For the top 10 players on the LPGA tour, the figure is about $700,000. Many players earn substantially more through product endorsements, appearance fees, and exhibitions.

In the United States, the top courses best known for hosting major tournaments include the Augusta National in Georgia, Pebble Beach in California, Oakmont and Merion in Pennsylvania, Oakland Hills in Michigan, Inverness in Ohio, and Pinehurst in North Carolina.

Some of the renowned courses in other countries include Royal Melbourne and Kingston Heath in Australia; St. Andrews, Royal Dornoch, Turnberry, and Muirfield in Scotland; and Royal County Down, Royal Portrush, and Ballybunion in Ireland.

chapter eight

TENNIS

Tennis at the pro level is a game of power, finesse, speed, savvy, stamina, concentration, and most importantly, confidence. "Confidence is the thing in tennis," observed the great champion Rod Laver. "[It] separates athletes of similar ability."

With just two players competing on the court, thousands of stadium spectators watch while mounds of money and prestige hang in the balance. The intense pressure can crack the most stalwart, and the slightest slip in confidence often leads to defeat.

The Basics

Most televised tennis matches are "singles," played by two people. "Doubles," a fascinating variation, is played by four.

For singles, the court measures 78 feet long by 27 feet wide (see Figure 43). It is divided in half by a yard-high net, with a player on either side. For doubles, the court's total width is increased by nine feet, and two players play as a team on each side.

There are men's singles and doubles, and women's singles and doubles. In addition, there is mixed doubles, in which each team is composed of a man and a woman.

Each player uses a tightly strung racket (or racquet) to hit the pressurized rubber ball back and forth across the net.

The object of the game is to keep hitting the ball over the net and into the opponent's court until the opponent fails to return it—by

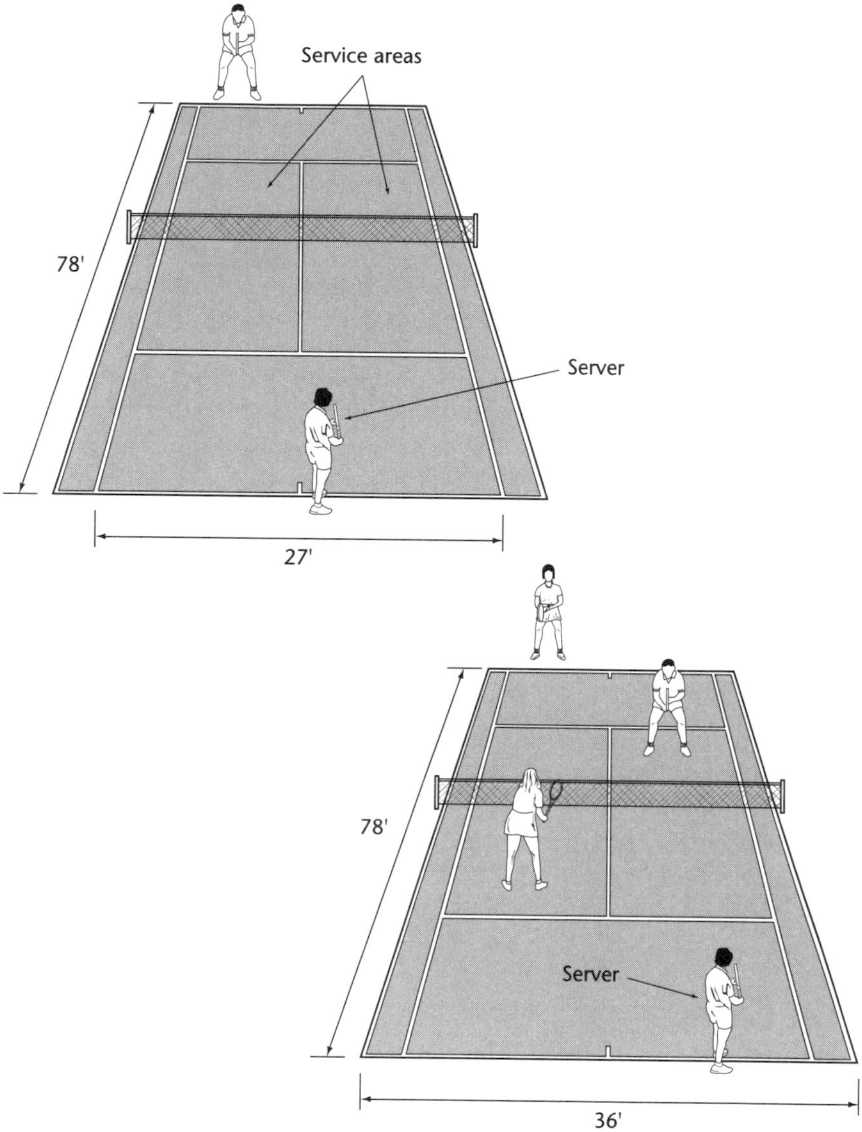

Figure 43. For singles (above left), the court is 78 feet long and 27 feet wide. For doubles (above right), its width is expanded to 36 feet. The net is three-and-a-half feet tall at the sides and sags in the middle to three feet.

Singles serve: To serve to an opponent in singles, the server stands just behind the baseline to the right of the center mark and must hit the ball into the service area ("service box") diagonally across the net. For the next serve, he or she stands to the left of the center mark and serves into the other box. Serves alternate in this manner until one player wins the game.

Doubles serve: To serve in doubles, the same sequence is observed. The difference is that the server's partner and the opponent not receiving the serve usually position themselves aggressively at the net.

hitting the ball into the net, hitting it out-of-bounds, allowing the ball to bounce more than once on his side of the net before hitting it, or failing to hit it at all. Each time a player fails to keep the ball in play, the other player is awarded a point.

Each point begins with a "serve." The designated server stands at the baseline, tosses the ball a few feet above his or her head, then strikes it hard with the racket so that the ball clears the net and hits within one of two "service areas" on the opponent's side of the net. In men's tennis, a fast serve (called a "cannonball") travels about 115 to 130 mph; for women, 100 to 110 mph. The opponent attempts to "return serve" by hitting the ball back over the net. The server is allowed to hit a second serve if the first one fails to go into the service area; if both serves fail, then the server loses the point. Also, a serve must be repeated if the ball grazes the top of the net but goes into the service area. That's called a "let serve."

Once the ball has been served, a player can select to hit the ball in five basic ways: forehand, backhand, forehand volley, backhand volley, and overhead smash (see Figures 44, 45, and 46). By altering

Figure 44. For an effective groundstroke (either forehand or backhand), power is generated and transferred to the racket as the body untwists—especially as the hips and shoulders pivot toward the ball—and as the player's weight shifts to the forward foot.

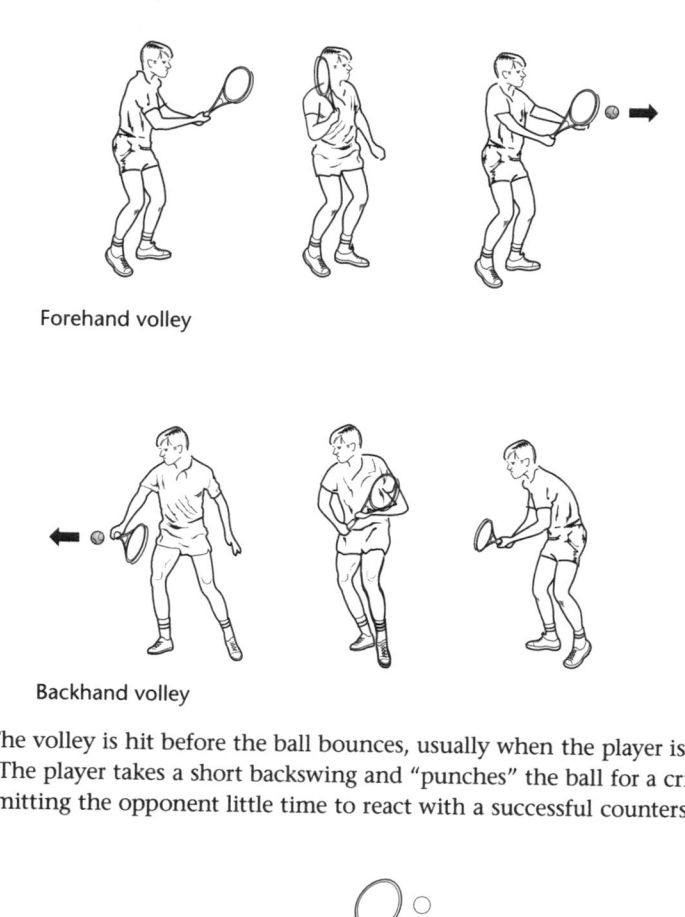

Forehand volley

Backhand volley

Figure 45. The volley is hit before the ball bounces, usually when the player is close to the net. The player takes a short backswing and "punches" the ball for a crisp return, permitting the opponent little time to react with a successful countershot.

Figure 46. The overhead smash is usually hit at the net in response to an opponent's attempt to hit a lob over the player's head. Hit hard with a serving motion, the overhead is a spectacular shot to watch and usually difficult for the opponent to return because of its velocity.

the way he swings the racket, he can also impart various spins to the ball to gain tactical advantage and to confuse the opponent. Topspin tends to make the ball follow a sharply arched trajectory and bounce up aggressively off the court. Underspin, or a "slice," slows the ball and, once it hits the court, tends to subdue its bounce and keep it low.

Scoring

The scoring in tennis is a bit eccentric but easy to follow:

A competition (or "match") comprises three subunits: points, games, and sets. To win a game, a player must earn four points (but win by two). To win a set, a player must win six games (but win by two). To win a match, a player must win two out of three sets (in some tournaments, three out of five sets). A good match usually takes about two hours.

Greatest tennis match ever? Some say it was the 3-hour, 53-minute Wimbledon finals played on July 5, 1980. In this superbly played five-set match, the Swede Bjorn Borg narrowly prevailed against American John McEnroe to win his fifth straight Wimbledon title. The score of this epic nail-biter was 1–6, 7–5, 6–3, 6–7 (18–16), 8–6.

If a set becomes tied at six games apiece, a "tiebreaker" is played. In a tiebreaker, the first player to win seven points (and win by two points) wins the set. In some championship matches, a tiebreaker is not used for the final set. Instead, play continues until one player wins that set by two games.

Game

A match begins with a coin toss; the winner of the toss can choose to serve or to receive serve for the first game. After that, each player serves for a complete game on an alternating basis. In doubles, each team serves for a complete game on an alternating basis. The teammates alternate serving, too, with each serving for an entire game (refer to Figure 43).

As mentioned, a player must win four points to win a game, but he or she has to win by a margin of two points. For example, if both players have won three points, either player will capture the game if he wins the next two points.

Scoring terminology is unusual. Having no points is called "love" (from the French word for "egg"). A player's first point is "15"; the second is "30"; the third is "40"; and the fourth wins the game. For example, if Player A is serving and has lost the first two points to his opponent, the score is "love–30." The server's score is always stated first. Player A wins the next point, so the score becomes 15–30. Player B wins the next; score is 15–40. (If Player B wins the next point or the point after that, he wins that game.) Player A must now win the next two points just to tie at 40–40; if that happens, then either player can win but only by a margin of two points.

If the game score becomes tied at 40–40 (referred to as "deuce"), then whichever player wins the next point is said to have "advantage." If the player with advantage proceeds to lose the following point, then the score reverts to deuce; if he wins that point, he wins that game.

Most experts consider 15–30 to be a critical juncture in a game. The next point will either tie the score at 30–30 or put one player at 15–40, within a point of winning the game.

Set

As a match progresses, the scoreboard is updated according to the scores for each set. For example, at the conclusion of a highly competitive match, the scoreboard might show:

Player A	6	6	7
Player B	2	7	5

In this best-of-three-sets match, Player A won the first set 6–2, lost the second 6–7 (a tiebreaker determined that set, which had been tied at six games apiece), and won the final set 7–5 (the players were tied at 5–5, and Player A won the next two games).

The seventh game of a set is often pivotal, according to experts, particularly if the score is 4–2 or 5–l. If, after six games, the score is

4–2, then the next game will either make the score close at 4–3 or place one player at 5–2, within a game of winning the set. The game after 5–1 will either complete the set at 6–1 or permit the other player to hang on at 5–2.

Styles of Play

Most singles players are, essentially, either "baseliners" or "net rushers."

Playing most points from behind the baseline, the baseliner used to be associated with a defensive style of play. This style was built upon shotmaking consistency and the ability to doggedly run down and return most shots hit by opponents. With the advancements of larger, more powerful metal and composite rackets over the past 25 years, a new breed of player—the offensive baseliner—thrives today and fires hard topspin shots from the baseline that travel deep into the opponent's court.

The net rusher, on the other hand, plays the traditional game of attack that has thrilled spectators for a century. At virtually every opportunity, this player aggressively rushes to the net in order to hit the ball before it bounces (a "volley"). He usually runs to the net after hitting a particularly good serve or a hard, penetrating groundstroke (either forehand or backhand) in order to hit a decisive volley. This bold, offensive style of play demands the utmost confidence, excellent hand-eye coordination, and very quick reflexes (see Figure 47).

Strategy

> "Never give your opponent a chance to make a shot he likes. . . . I may sound unsporting when I claim that the primary object of tennis is to break up your opponent's game, but it is my honest belief that no man is defeated until his game is crushed, or at least weakened. Nothing so upsets a man's mental and physical poise as to be continually led into error."
>
> —*William T. Tilden,* Match Play and the Spin of the Ball, *1925*

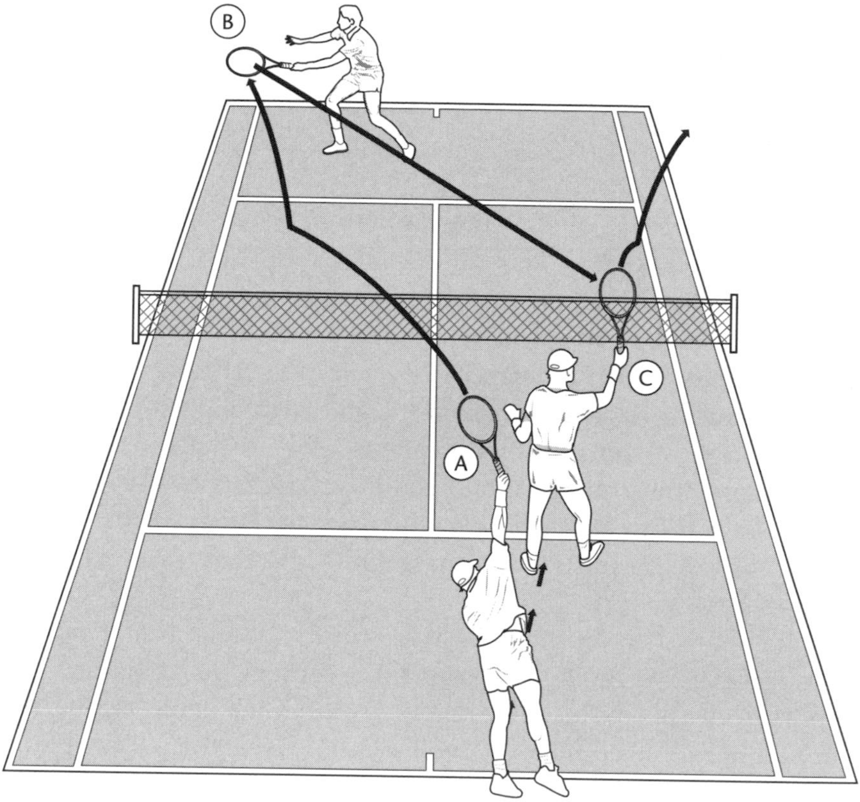

Figure 47. The aggressive serve-and-volley tactic often confines a point to just three shots: (a) the serve, (b) the opponent's return, and (c) the server's put-away volley while rushing to the net. This offensive style has been the stock-in-trade for many of the sport's greatest champions. To combat it, an exceptionally well-placed return of serve is necessary.

This was the strategy Tilden used to dominate the world of tennis throughout the 1920s. The same strategy was employed to perfection by Arthur Ashe in winning the 1975 Wimbledon trophy over Jimmy Connors, by John McEnroe and Martina Navratilova to rule the game in the '80s, by Pete Sampras throughout the '90s, and by many, many other champions.

In the finals of the 1920 U.S. Championships at Forest Hills, New York, "Little Bill" Johnston was defeated in five sets by "Big Bill" Tilden, who went on to win five more national titles in consecutive order (each time against Johnston!). During that match, a news airplane stalled over the stadium and crashed just outside the gates. The stunned players, who had felt the court tremble beneath their feet, were instructed by the umpire to play on.

A long-standing maxim in tennis is "Never change a winning game; always change a losing one." Champions such as Tilden, Ashe, McEnroe, Navratilova, and Sampras mastered the complete array of tennis shots and, therefore, had the capability to alter their playing styles for strategic advantage.

If, for example, their opponents preferred to hit with topspin, champions such as these would cut or slice their shots so the ball would skid and stay low to the ground—a difficult ball to hit with topspin. If their opponents preferred to bang it out from the baseline, these accomplished tacticians would hit soft, short balls to draw their opponents to the net where they would be forced to play in uncomfortable territory. If opponents liked to hit forehand shots, they would hit to their backhand side.

There are, certainly, several notable champions who never altered their playing style for tactical reasons. Bjorn Borg, for example, who was the major force in the late '70s and early '80s, gained tremendous success by adhering to his unorthodox topspin game played from the baseline. Jimmy Connors and Steffi Graf stuck tenaciously to their hard-hitting baseline games, too, as they blasted paths to victory.

For spectators, some of the more exciting matches are those in which a talented player is slipping toward defeat. It's thrilling and instructive to observe how that player seeks to turn the tide, usually by first struggling to regain his or her confidence and concentration and then by making smart tactical changes in his game. The record books are punctuated with memorable matches in which versatile players snatched victory from the jaws of defeat through determination, cool calculation, creative shotmaking, and resourcefulness.

In addition to factoring in the opponent's strengths and weaknesses, the court surface has a significant bearing on a player's choice of strategy and style of play. There are three basic types of court—hard surface, clay, and grass:

- *Hard surface:* Most hard-surface courts are made with an asphalt or cement base, then topped with an acrylic or synthetic fiber coating. Generally, these surfaces make for fast-paced tennis and favor hard hitters. (For indoor matches, synthetic matting is usually used; it slows down the ball.)
- *Clay:* Clay and claylike surfaces are the softest and slowest; they favor a defensive baseline style of play. The surface tends to reduce the effectiveness of aggressive, hard-hitting players because it slows down the ball. Net rushers are jeopardized because on clay the opponent has more time to hit effective passing shots. It is best suited for patient baseliners whose arsenal includes a variety of spins and finesse shots.
- *Grass:* Nowadays, very few tournaments are played on this venerable surface, the fastest, trickiest, and least predictable of all. Hard-hit shots tend to skid on this fast surface and stay low. Softly hit shots barely bounce, and backspin makes the ball stay very low. Also, the natural unevenness of grass makes the ball take unexpected bounces. It is best suited for players who hit hard serves and immediately rush the net to volley the returns.

Doubles

Tactically, there are noteworthy differences between singles and doubles because doubles involves four players instead of two and because the court is nine feet wider (the extra space along each side is called the "alley").

A doubles match is usually won by the team that makes the fewest errors and dominates the net. To achieve this, the two teammates must rush the net at every opportunity and be able to hit excellent volleys and overhead smashes.

The most effective shots in doubles are usually either sharply angled toward the sidelines (to take full advantage of the extra playing area) or hit low and straight down the middle of the court and between the opponents (these shots often cause opponents a fatal moment of hesitation in deciding who should hit the ball).

High-arching shots called lobs are often hit in doubles to force the net players back to the baseline. Players at the net, therefore, often attempt to intercept a lob with an overhead smash. An effective, well-placed lob can quickly reverse the dynamics of a point by forcing the opponents at the net to retreat to the baseline, thereby giving the team that lobbed the ball a good chance to commandeer the net positions.

Equipment

Except for the racket, tennis equipment is unremarkable—a short-sleeved shirt, shorts or skirt, socks, tennis shoes, and a Dacron (or nylon)-and-wool-covered rubber ball two and a half inches in diameter.

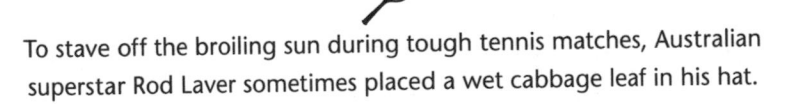

To stave off the broiling sun during tough tennis matches, Australian superstar Rod Laver sometimes placed a wet cabbage leaf in his hat.

Technologically, the racket has radically transformed itself from the various wooden models used for the first 100 years of the game. In the late 1960s, metal rackets initiated the wooden models' march toward extinction. In the ensuing years, lighter, stronger materials and design refinements that enlarged the racket face and hitting surface have significantly enhanced the racket's performance—in both control and power. John McEnroe was the last player to reach the finals of Wimbledon using a wooden racket. That was in 1982 (when he was beaten by Jimmy Connors). Most pros play with rackets made of graphite that measure about 29 inches long and 12 inches wide.

The best strings are still made of a very traditional material called "gut"—actually twisted strands of sheep or cow intestines. These strings are woven very tightly across the racket face with a tension of 60 to 80 pounds. Most pros claim that gut is unsurpassed in providing control, power, and finesse, or "feel."

Other Important Stuff

Ace: A serve so fast and well placed that the opponent can't even touch the ball with his or her racket, much less return it.

Backcourt: The area between the service line and baseline.

Changeover: This occurs after every odd-numbered game. The players switch sides.

Crosscourt: A shot hit diagonally across the court.

Fault: If the first serve fails to hit in the service area, it is declared a "fault." If the second serve also fails, that is a "double fault," and the server loses that point.

Match point: The point which, if won by the player in the lead, wins the match.

Poach: In doubles, the player at the net "poaches" the ball when he suddenly crosses to his partner's side of the court to intercept and hit the return. This aggressive tactic can catch the opposing team off guard, but it often leaves an area of the court unprotected that the opposition can exploit.

Service break (or break): When a player wins a game that his or her opponent served. This is a serious setback for the player whose serve was broken (because a player should have the upper hand when serving) and will eventually cause that player to lose the set unless he can "break back."

History

Tennis is one of the few sports that can trace its genesis to a specific person, place, and date. At an English garden party in 1873, a British army officer named Walter C. Wingfield introduced a lawn game which he had adapted mostly from the medieval sport of court tennis. Four years later, in 1877, the first championship (men's singles only) for "lawn tennis" was held at the All-England Croquet Club in the London suburb of Wimbledon.

The new game of tennis quickly replaced croquet as England's most popular outdoor sport (and prompted the croquet club in Wimbledon to alter its priorities and its name).

Lawn tennis's precursor, court tennis, came out of the Middle Ages, when it was played in the courtyards of French monasteries and later the courtyards of French châteaus and English castles. Still played today in a very few places in England, France, and the United States, court tennis is a complicated racket sport played across a net and against the surrounding walls.

Over the years, the manicured grass courts of Wimbledon have become tennis's hallowed ground and site of its most renowned annual championships. The club instituted the men's doubles championship in 1879, women's singles in 1884, and both women's doubles and mixed doubles in 1913.

The sport caught on quickly in the United States, too. The U.S. Tennis Association (USTA) was founded in 1881 to function as the sport's governing body, and its international counterpart, the International Tennis Federation (ITF), was organized in 1913.

When Dick Williams and Karl Behr faced each other in the quarterfinal round of the 1914 U.S. Nationals, they had more in common than the desire to win a tennis tournament. Two years before, both had survived the sinking of the *Titanic.*

Steeped in tradition, several of the most revered tennis championships have long histories. The first U.S. Open championship (played each year in Flushing Meadows, New York; hard surface courts) was held in 1881; women's play was included in 1887. The French Open (held annually in Paris; red clay courts—technically, red brick dust) was begun in 1891. The Australian Open (held in Melbourne; hard surface courts) was initiated in 1905. Because of the stiff competition and various court surfaces, it's a very rare accomplishment for a male or female player to win all four of the biggest tournaments (Wimbledon, U.S. Open, French Open, and Australian Open) in one calendar year—a feat called a "Grand Slam."

Helen Wills Moody, an extraordinary player of the 1920s and 1930s, never had a formal tennis lesson. In addition to winning 31 Grand Slam tournaments and two Olympic gold medals, she was an accomplished painter and author.

The Davis Cup—an annual men's competition composed of national teams from around the world—dates back to 1900. The comparable competition for women is the Fed Cup (formally the Federation Cup), begun in 1963.

A milestone decision for the sport came in 1968 when the ITF and its member organizations voted to open the major tournaments to pros as well as amateurs (thus U.S. "Open," and so on). Before that, only amateurs were permitted to play in the major championships. Since then, the professional players have dominated the game and now enjoy sizable paychecks for winning. Top men and women players earn more than $1 million a year in prize money (a few earn several times that amount), plus whatever they make from product endorsements, appearance fees, and exhibition matches.

The Women's Tennis Association Tour (WTA Tour), which annually sanctions about 55 tournaments around the world, traces its origins back to 1970. The men's Association of Tennis Professionals Tour (ATP Tour), which evolved from the ATP (begun in 1972), sanctions nearly 80 annual tournaments worldwide. The best players usually enter 15 to 20 of the WTA or ATP Tour tournaments a year, plus the Grand Slam tournaments and, during the off-season, a few exhibition matches.

INDEX

ABOUT THE AUTHOR

Dan Bartges is the author of *Winter Olympics Made Simple.* He has been interviewed for his sports insights and informative synopses by CNN and radio stations throughout the United States, Canada, and as far away as Japan and Australia. He began his career in 1972 as the editorial writer and cartoonist for the *Alexandria Gazette* (Virginia) and later became a freelance writer and photographer for the *Washington Post, New York Post,* and others. For 13 years he worked for The Martin Agency, a leading advertising and marketing firm, most recently as a senior vice president and management supervisor. A graduate of Hampden-Sydney College and the University of Richmond, Bartges resides in Richmond, Virginia, with his wife, daughter, and passel of pets. He now divides his time writing, painting, consulting, and at-home parenting.